To Stephen

L.

GW01396273

g

Bill

Christmas 1989.

x x x.

HEAVY WEATHER WINDSURFING

Jürgen Hönscheid/Ken Winner

Heavy Weather Windsurfing

On Funboards and Sinkers

STANFORD MARITIME
LONDON

The authors and publisher wish to thank
Uwe Preuss, who after Jürgen Hönscheid's
serious accident worked with him on several
parts of this text. The content, editing and
layout of this book owe much to his
collaboration.
We also wish to thank Dominique Merz for
his marvellous photographs of Ken Winner's
technique.

Stanford Maritime Limited
Member Company of the George Philip Group
12–14 Long Acre   London WC2E 9LP
Editor Phoebe Mason

First published in Great Britain 1984
English edition © Stanford Maritime Ltd 1984

English translation by Nick King and Uwe Preuss

Originally published as *Starkwind Windsurfen*
Copyright © Buchheim Editions SA, Fribourg 1984
and Mosaik Verlag GmbH, München

Set in 10/10½ Monophoto Univers 689 by
Tameside Filmsetting Limited
Ashton-under-Lyne, Lancashire

Cover photo by Christian Le Bozec
Photos in text by Yves Buchheim,
Dominique Merz, Dieter Menne, Daniel
Forster, Christian Petit, Cliff Webb,
Syltbild Stöver

Printed and bound in Switzerland by
Zobrist & Hof AG, 4410 Liestal

Contents

Jürgen Hönscheid

Jürgen is one of the superstars of windsurfing, and has been so almost from the very beginning. When he had his bad accident in the autumn of 1983 he was the favourite to win the World Cup, and had of course won numerous Funboard competitions.

It would be wrong to measure his importance in windsurfing only by his racing success, however: Jürgen has never been interested in triangle races. His career started with the first wave-riding competitions. He is one of those who have pushed the techniques and equipment to its limits, and whose ideas have brought windsurfing to the standard we enjoy today.

Born 1954
Residence: Westerland, Sylt, Germany
Major regattas:
1980 Pan Am Cup—2nd
1983 Pan Am Cup—3rd
1982 World speed record, Weymouth
Major sponsor: F2

Ken Winner

Ken is recognized as one of the best all-round windsurfers in the world. He has competed in all its different aspects at international level, with enormous success. For example, in the Windsurfer World Cup that he won in 1980 he dominated all three disciplines—freestyle, long-distance racing and pentathlon.

Ken is known as one of the most accurate World Cup professionals, who concentrates on consistency and detail, concerning equipment as much as technique, strategy and tactics. Thus he is, like Jürgen, one of the greats who even if he once steps down from racing will continue to be a star.

Born 1955
Residence: Annapolis, Maryland U.S.A.
Major regattas:
1980 Windsurfer World Cup—1st
1981 Pan Am World Cup—1st
1982 Euro-Funboard Cup—1st
1983 World Cup—2nd
Major sponsors:
   Bic Marine
   Jantzen Sportswear
   North Sails
   O'Neill Wetsuits

Introduction

Windsurfing, probably the sport which has had the most explosive development of any, has expanded in the last ten years to offer a wide range of variations. Anyone deciding to take it up thus has to consider almost from the start in what direction he wishes to learn and perhaps specialize. There is a choice of four broad areas:
—racing on classic triangular Olympic-type courses
—freestyle windsurfing
—funboard sailing
—touring.
The decision will be influenced by the possibilities and conditions that exist in his areas as well as the time and money at his disposal. At present, competitions, equipment manufacturers and designers, magazines and advertising all concentrate on funboard sailing. This also applies to most competent boardsailors now, and we professionals in the competition circuit also promote it, of course. We believe that funboard sailing epitomizes the special qualities of windsurfing. However, you will soon see in several of these chapters that we certainly don't describe only our own specialities.

We made our decisions early. I, Jürgen, am familiar with surf-boarding from childhood, and was probably one of the first to bring the design and construction of surf-riding boards to the sport of windsurfing. I came second in the first Pan Am Cup in Hawaii with such a board (and was allowed to call myself World Champion).

I, Ken, only started funboard sailing later, after racing my Windsurfer Rocket in triangular-course events, and after freestyle windsurfing. After reaching a peak in the 1980 World Championships (first in Freestyle, Long Distance and Pentathlon) I went over entirely to funboard sailing – which has also brought a few titles.

If you have already decided on funboard sailing, when learning start from the beginning on boards of this type. This will make the early stages easier, and it is also easier to improve to an advanced level on funboards. The first board you buy should also be of this type.

This brings us to a serious question: which board should you buy? If you are a beginner, this is fairly easy. You are starting from the beginning and need a robustly built and stable all-round funboard. It is more difficult when you have advanced further. The problem then lies in estimating how advanced you are, so that you can select appropriate equipment. Advertising is not much help as it gives the impression that almost every board is suitable for anyone and under any conditions. Therefore, in this book we use a classification system similar to that which has proved successful in skiing, and is also used as a buying aid by some good sailboard manufacturers. It is known as the BASE system:

B stands for Beginner, the apprentice windsurfer.

A is the all-round sailor, the practised average person for whom windsurfing is one of several sports. He accepts difficult conditions, but does not seek them out.

S is the sporting windsurfer, who seeks out tough conditions, is more specialized and chooses his equipment accordingly.

E is the expert, the extreme windsurfer and specialist, who favours particular, often extreme, conditions and whose equipment is specifically suited to this use.

The BASE concept can be understood as an equipment buying aid, but it is more than that. In the chapters on skills we have tried to match the various board shapes to the particular movements and manoeuvres to which they are suited, and which are easily learned and sailed on such boards. After all, different sailors need different boards, and different boards need modified sailing techniques and more or less skill while offering varying safety.

You can therefore use the BASE system as an aid to estimating your own ability and also as a path on which to learn.

We also hope that it is a contribution to safety in funboard sailing, which schools and instructors in the sport, and the lifesaving and rescue organizations, will welcome.

In this book we do not go into the basic aspects of windsurfing. In our opinion there is already enough literature for the beginner, and in any case it is worthwhile learning the basic skills in a good school.

From Beginner to Sinker Pilot

TYPES OF FUNBOARD

For many years windsurfers have struggled with equipment that is unsuitable for strong winds. Not only do high winds and waves test their ability, but also poorly trimmed and balanced equipment. The advent of the first planing boards with retractable centreboard, flat planing surface, two or three skegs and in some cases footstraps, which for the first time allowed the true excitement of high-speed downwind sailing, heightened the enjoyment of the sport. These boards were called 'funboards'. Nowadays there are funboards for every possible purpose:
—All-round use and racing
—Slalom racing
—Speed sailing
—Sailing and jumping in breaking waves.
These boards are classified according to their buoyancy as floaters, semi-floaters (marginals) or sinkers. The decision in favour of a particular design depends above all on the intended use, the winds that can be expected and the type of sailing area, and on the weight and ability of the sailor.

All-round/Racing Funboards
Beginners and all-rounders
Funboard competitions are designed as testing courses for these boards. Short upwind legs are combined with long downwind and reaching legs, and with reaching and gybing slaloms. Boards are required here which beat upwind well but are also extremely fast and manoeuvrable.

Other important requirements are:
—sufficient volume
—good acceleration and easy sailing
—low weight despite sound, strong construction
—easy, predictable handling under all conditions, particularly in the swell.
These are all characteristics which are required of a good funboard. Competition results are therefore more helpful than the tests in some windsurfing magazines. A board which often wins races will also be enjoyable when not racing, in leisure sailing, provided it handles well.

Technical data

Length	330–390 cm according to weight and ability
Beam	60–72 cm
Thickness	12–16 cm
Scoop	23–28 cm
Rocker	none
Weight	not more than 16 kg

Beam 30 cm from stern: 29–34 cm
Retractable centreboard ca. 65 cm long, turning axis usually 150 cm from the stern.

Mast track and daggerboard must be easily adjustable while under way.
Skeg: one
Stern shape: usually a rounded pintail

The underwater hull of these boards usually has a pronounced Vee-shape, which is somewhat rounded towards the bow. The Vee is now often combined with a double concave bottom surface for even better acceleration and planing characteristics. The length of the flat planing surface, seen from the side, is about 190 cm. 100 cm from the stern, the sharp outer edge is slowly drawn inwards and runs forward as a so-called tucked-under edge. The deck is sharply cambered in order to combine sufficient volume with optimum rail. This also increases the stiffness of the board and makes it

more comfortable to stand on. The fully retractable centreboard should not project above the deck. The widest point of the board is just in front of the mid-point of the overall length. The edge outline (seen in plan view) should appear harmonious, since the old rule usually applies: *What looks right, sails right.* Towards the stern, the outline is a compromise between speed and manoevrability.

Slalom Funboard
All-round and sporting sailors
The slalom board is a more specialized design, which is also used in competitions such as ins and outs (slalom) in the Funboard Cup series.

The ideal board is extremely fast and easily controlled on all reaching courses, and at the many gybe marks goes through the turn with a min-

imum loss of speed and quickly resumes planing. It must be possible to jump, gybe and make the best possible use of the waves while retaining full control. Pure sinkers are

Jürgen's World Cup boards. From left: 1–3, high wind wave-riders 240 × 50 cm, wide tail, needle nose; 4, waveboard for light winds 255 × 58 cm. 5 and 6 are experimental asymmetrics for waves from the left (5) and right (6); they are shorter and wider than normal asymmetrics used in small waves. 7, slalom funboard 300 × 65 cm for light winds. 8, slalom board 265 × 56 cm for average conditions. 9–11, guns of 280, 230 and 250 cm for speed and extreme conditions in slalom and wave-riding competition.

very seldom used. For most advanced sailors slalom boards are the most suitable designs and can be used everywhere in breakers and open water in strong winds.

Technical data

Length	250–330 cm according to sailor's weight and ability and the wind strength
Beam	50–65 cm
Thickness	ca. 12 cm
Scoop	ca. 15–25 cm
Rocker	max. 1.5 cm
Weight	not more than 10 kg

Beam 30 cm from stern: 27–34 cm
Volume: generally floater or semi-sinker
Stern shape: pintail or pintail winger
Mast rail and footstraps arranged for reaching courses and sailing with the wind on the beam.
Skegs: one large single fin, often with two relatively small outer thrusters.

The underwater hull is sharply Veed, at least towards the stern, usually combined with a double concave bottom. The tucked-under edge runs along the whole length of the board. There is also a long, almost flat section in the planing surface area. If there is any rocker, it should run smoothly and not abruptly.
—The less the rocker, the quicker the board will be with the wind abeam.
—The more the rocker, the more easily the board can be controlled on reaching courses.
The widest point is usually at half the length. The stern is shaped for manoeuvrability, control and speed. Wings on the tail often give a final grip for radical gybes. This size of board manages without any daggerboard, since skeg pressure alone can be used to sail sufficiently well to windward.

Speed Boards *Experts*

In order to master the giant waves of Waimea Bay, Sunset Beach and the pipeline, the Hawaiian surf-riders long ago developed the correct specialized boards, so-called 'guns'. The main requirement for this purpose is 100 per cent control at high speed, as in riding such a wave the board receives an overdose of power. Falls can have serious results. Typical characteristics of a gun are:
—a long-drawn outline (in plan view) with little curvature in the rear half
—a lot of rocker
—one skeg and a very narrrow stern which runs to a point
—maximum width nearer the bow.
In 1980 Hugh England, Derk Thijs and possibly other surfers discovered that guns with a sail must also be the ideal equipment for speed trials. Because of control problems a certain top speed could not be exceeded, however. Hugh England tried a gun in the Laalaea Speed Trials at Maui; Derk Thijs used one to race over the course in the Smirnoff Cup on Fehmarn. At that time, however, sailing techniques and rigs were not sufficiently developed and the guns were put aside for a time. The design was only recalled at the start of the era of sinkers, short-boom rigs, power gybing and water starts. Phillip Pudenz, for example, bought a surfboard of this type in a surf shop on the North Shore in Hawaii, built in footstraps and a mast step, and used it to sail an official world record.

Technical data

Length	240–300 cm
Beam	47–55 cm according to length
Thickness	7–10 cm max., usually at the widest point
Scoop	15–25 cm
Rocker	1.5–3.5 cm
Weight	under 10 kg

Beam 30 cm from the stern: 18–28 cm
Volume: semi-sinker or sinker
Stern shape: usually sharp pintail
Skeg: one, large enough for control
Hull underwater: usually Vee-shape in section, slightly rounded towards the bow.
Guns are designed above all for broad-reaching courses in extremely high winds. With the wind abeam they are relatively slow. The best boards have more lift in the stern area through a concave bottom, more beam and less rocker. Such lift would, however, be a disadvantage on a reach: the stern rises too high, the bow is thereby lowered, and the rails in the bow area can dig in and slew off uncontrollably. The rails in the stern area no longer grip and the board can slide sideways.

It is possible to sail to windward with guns, but only within certain limits. For speed trials the future probably lies with asymmetrical designs.

Breaker Boards *Experts*

The most important characteristic of a good breaking-waves board is excellent manoeuvrability. However, you also need perfect control when jumping wave-riding or making sudden turns. The board must accelerate quickly and cope with high speeds over short periods. Specialists need different boards for different wave conditions.

The boards described below give only a general picture. The final choice of stern shape and skeg arrangement depends on your sailing style, preferences and ability.

Different sea conditions:

1 Low swell—light wind
0.5–2.5 m   Force 3–5
2 Low swell—high wind
0.5–2.5 m   Force 6–9
3 High swell—light wind
2.5 m–?   Force 3–5
4 High swell—high wind
2.5 m–?   Force 6–9

The following descriptions cover typical characteristics that a board should ideally have for these different conditions. There are of course all-round solutions, compromises which are more or less usable under most conditions, but they can never be perfect for a particular day.

1 Low swell—light wind

In these conditions, which are the most common, the following points in the board's design are most important:

—It must be possible to use a large sail (ca. 5.7 sq m).
—There must be enough volume and dynamic lift to ensure that the board will not sink in momentary lulls, but will glide through.
—An adjustable mast track is certainly an advantage: when trimmed back the rig can be pulled up using the uphaul line; trimmed forward the board will plane earlier and cross breaking waves more easily.
—Early starting and excellent acceleration are important, as the waves are often not very far apart and speed for manoeuvres and jumps must be built up between them. A double-concave bottom or outer channel is therefore often used.
—Three-skeg thruster or four-skeg arrangement, in order to sail sufficiently well upwind and to have enough grip for all eventualities. Skegs as parallel as possible as angled skegs have a braking effect.
—Tucked-under edge for quick planing and good sideways cut-off in sharp turns.

—Needle nose and low volume in the bow area make the board more sensitive and manoeuvrable, which is often required in this type. Also gives less rail grip towards the bow.

—The propulsive power in riding waves comes equally from the waves and the wind. In order to sail a good 'bottom turn' or 'off the lip', for example, you need maximum speed coming out of the wave, which can only be obtained with a relatively wide planing surface towards the stern of the board.

Length   250–300 cm
Beam   54–65 cm
Thickness   10–13 cm
Floater/Semi-sinker

2 Low swell—high wind

Since a strong wind will always lead to a choppy sea, the board must sail more smoothly than the type described in category 1, and have better handling. It needs less volume and dynamic lift. However, it should be a size too large rather than too small, as many people spoil their fun in sailing with boards which are too small.

—The widest point and greatest volume are farther forward.
—The rails are thinner and run in a sharper radius.
—The outline is less rounded at the stern.
—The additional skegs are smaller, the main skeg larger.
—The tucked-under edge runs farther inwards and towards the stern.

Length	210–265 cm
Beam	50–60 cm
Thickness	8–13 cm
Semi-sinker/Sinker	

3 High swell—light wind

For these conditions you need a board with an outline like a gun, only slightly wider and with a little more volume. It must not sink, as heavy breakers with a gusty wind of Force 3 to 5 often contain lulls with light wind or none at all. One must also cross mountains of foam and use the momentum when descending a wave while retaining full control.

Length	250–300 cm
Beam	50–60 cm
Thickness	10–13 cm
Floater/Semi-sinker	

Two boards from Jürgen's collection: a gun with the widest part well forward and a long, nearly straight, tapering outline to the tail (right), and a 'loose' board for smaller waves.

4 High swell—high wind

In these 'survival conditions' sinkers with the gun shape are used. Large boards would be really dangerous here: in jumping they offer too large a surface to the wind; in riding down waves they become 'nervous' and start vibrating.

Length	210–270 cm
Beam	49–60 cm
Thickness	8–12 cm

Sinker with narrow rails, sharp pintail, sometimes with wings. A slightly heavier board is often no disadvantage and allows more robust construction.

Asymmetrical Boards

These designs are particularly suited to areas with reliable conditions, i.e. steady wind strength and a dominant direction. Matt Schweitzer, one of the first sailors to successfully use asymmetrical boards, could hardly use his 'wind-from-the-right' Hookipa board on Diamond Head, where the wind is usually from the left.

The design of these boards also concentrates on the ability to ride

Fin arrangement on Jürgen's 'wave from the left' board. The thruster fin is also asymmetric.

15

back in on the surf. They only really work where the swell runs independently of the wind and in a regular pattern over a well-shaped sandbank or reef. The wind must blow consistently from one side, relative to the breaker direction.

The outline of these designs combines the advantages described in the section below on Outlines under Types A and B. One can, of course, combine a wide variety of different stern shapes, and also asymmetrical skeg and footstrap arrangements. The sections and rails are also asymmetrical.

Advantages:
—In sailing out through the waves there is enough beam and therefore dynamic lift to cross waves and accelerate quickly between them for high jumps.
—In riding a wave downwind there is enough control for a long, drawn-out bottom turn; then, however, a sensitive board for a super-quick cut-back with a tight radius or an extreme 'off the lip' turn.

Disadvantage:
—The board can only be used for the wind and wave direction for which it was designed.

Asymmetric 'wave from the left' board at work: the shorter, more curved side is on the inside towards the wave. It has sensitive reaction to foot-steering and allows very tight turns.

CONSTRUCTION FEATURES

The Outline

The plan-view outline of a board often receives insufficient attention in contrast to the stern and under-water hull shape. The outline is just as important for the sailing qualities, however. The following examples should make it clear which functions are influenced by the outline.

Board A is a speed board (gun) with a long, gradual curve. The maximum beam is forward of the mid-point of the length, so that in turning by shifting your weight more rail enters the water and guides the board through the turn. The turn follows a large radius but can be precisely controlled.

The narrow, gradually curved planing surface allows the board to climb far out of the water. The wetted surface area is then reduced, giving a high top speed.

The narrow stern prevents this part of the board climbing too far out of the water, so that the rails there continue to grip well. This allows:
—controlled planing in a straight line
—large-radius turns
—high top speed.

Board B has the widest point farther towards the stern and a large part of the total area in the planing surface. In the sternmost third there is a pronounced curve in the outline; the nose is relatively narrow. As a result the board turns almost on the spot; very little rail in the forward part can grip and you can sail very tight turns. In choppy water and high winds a board with this outline will be extremely restless and difficult to control, however, because it has less directional stability. This allows:

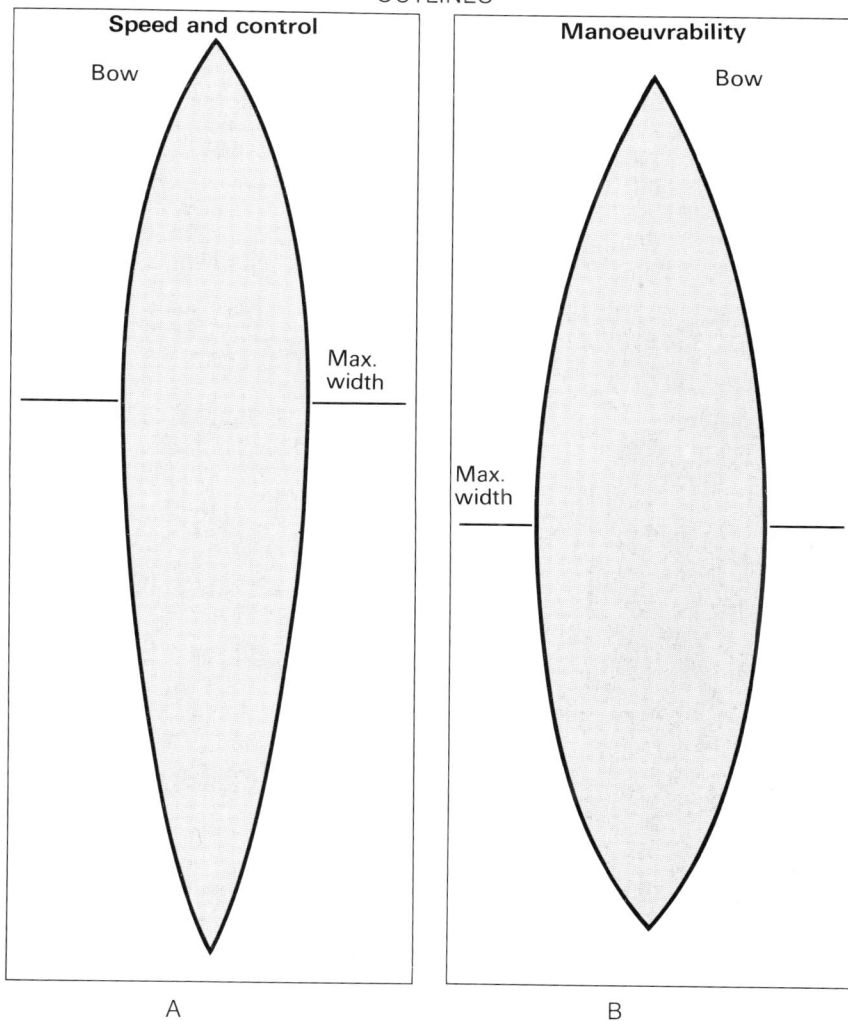

—quick acceleration, limited top speed
—very tight turns
—very sensitive handling.

Speed and control

Bow

Max. width

A

Manoeuvrability

Bow

Max. width

B

Bow and Stern Shapes

The controversy which has gone round in circles for years in surfing has now become established among boardsailors. Stern shapes change from year to year and there are hundreds of different views on this subject. On the one hand there are those who cannot have enough wings on their boards, while others sail only on classic and elegant pintails. Pintails and rounded pintails with two wings are most common, and certainly belong to the most tried and tested stern shapes.

Stern shapes can have a considerable effect on the following qualities:
—planing characteristics
—speed and the way the water leaves the board (drag)
—edge grip in turns
—manoeuvrability.

Wings are small, flat extensions intended to be immersed and grip in a turn as a sort of extra skeg. They also offer an elegant method of combining a narrow stern and a wide planing surface. Soft wings are more gradual steps which are not so effective. Wings often also extend under the board. Board C illustrates a board with double wings. F on the other hand is one of the most common stern designs, a pintail winger.

a **The Rounded Pintail** is designed to combine a wide beam with a lot of curve in the stern. It is a design for moderate winds and is often used in larger competition boards.

b **The Pure Pintail** is sharply pointed. It is not as manoeuvrable but offers controlled sailing in a straight line in high winds.

c **The Swallowtail** has plenty of rail in the water up to the final point in sharp turns, and therefore good handling. This design is a combination of pintail and squashtail.

Also called **Fishtail.**

d **The Squashtail** has a large planing area towards the stern and is therefore suited to light winds. This extra planing area, however, makes it difficult to control at high speeds and in choppy water.

e **The Diamondtail** has characteristics between those of swallow- and squashtail.

g A 'no nose' or 'needle nose' board. Long familiar to surf-riders, this bow shape is becoming increasingly popular on windsurfers shorter than 3 m for use in light and moderate winds. The lack of volume towards the bow makes the board less sluggish, and because of the narrow nose it has less rail grip towards the bow. It

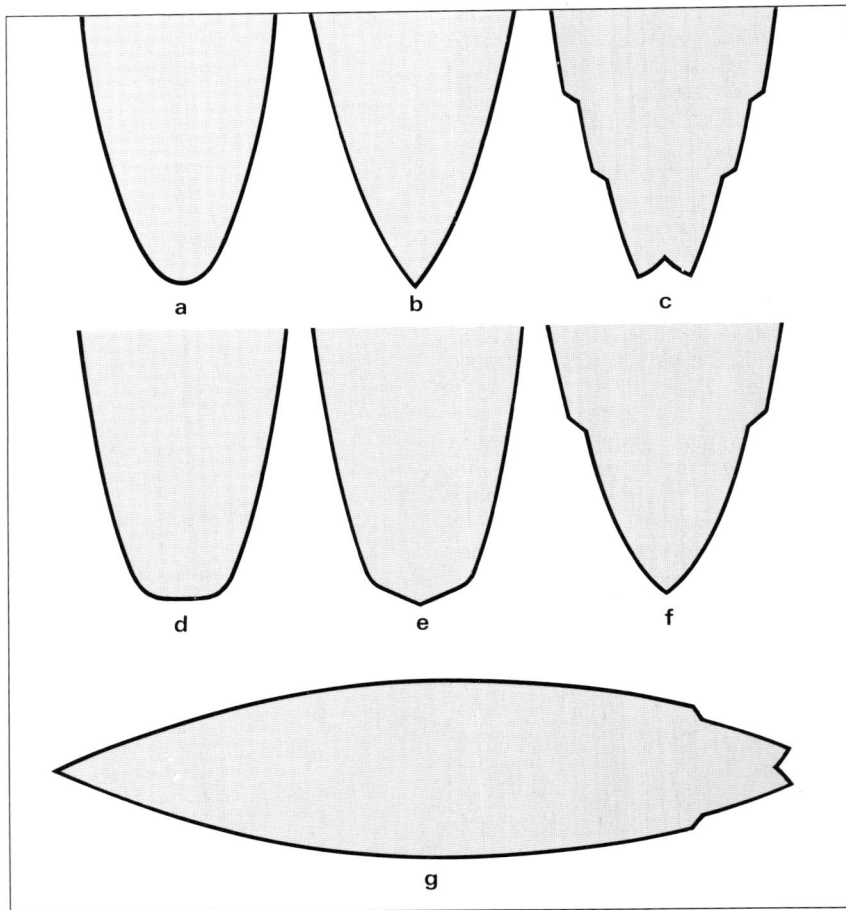

Tail and nose designs: a, rounded pintail; b, pintail; c, double-wing swallowtail; d, squashtail; e, diamond tail; f, pintail winger; g, swallowtail winger with needle nose.

becomes very sensitive and turns sharply over the planing area on a very short radius.

Whatever the form of the outline, it is very important to round off the point of the bow to a soft curve: sharp bows have caused serious injuries. Sailing qualities will not be affected.

Edge, Bottom and Deck Forms

a Edges with a tighter upper radius are sometimes used in the forward part of long boards in order to give better upwind qualities and a smoother reaction.

b Rounded rails make long boards more manoeuvrable, as they slide sideways more smoothly.

c Rails with the tighter lower radius are the most common; on short boards they are usually combined with a tucked-under edge. This is thin at the beginning, 30–40 cm from the stern, and then widens towards the centre of the board, thinning out again towards the bow.

d A full rail with a sharp edge gives good waterflow and the best possible effectiveness of the planing surface. Used towards the bow, it would tend to dig in and slew round, however.

e A thin rail with a sharp edge grips even in extremely tight turns. It is found at the stern to about 30–40 cm forward, going over in racing boards to rail D. On short boards the sharp edge is 'tucked under' as in rail C.

f Tucked-under edges were developed by surfers. They offer good sideways grip and water flow in quick manoeuvres without digging under. The tucked-under edge therefore runs the whole length of the board, its deepest point coinciding with the widest beam.

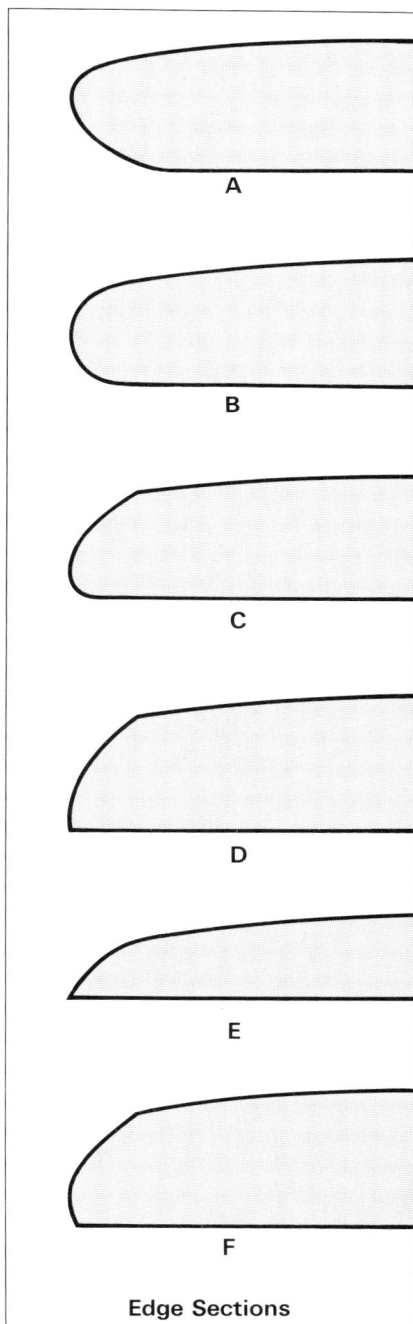

A

B

C

D

E

F

Edge Sections

Underwater shapes (see page 20)

1 The flat bottom allows the board to plane more quickly. It is usually used towards the bow of short boards and at the start of the planing area.

2 The Vee towards the stern keeps the middle skeg immersed and clear of any foam, allowing good steering with the feet and giving good handling and control. The underwater area is reduced with increased speed.

3 The rounded or bevelled section gives a smooth entry, improves upwind ability and is often found towards the bow of longer boards.

4 A concave bottom gives plenty of lift for quick reaction at around Force 4. It is usually at the start of the planing area.

5 The double concave bottom is very fast with the wind abeam. Placed towards the stern, it gives directional stability through the Vee in the middle and improves rail grip.

6 The Vee with dropped wings not only widens the outline sideways but the edges also stand out below. This gives a similar effect to the double concave but the edges grip even better.

7 The channel bottom has almost the same purpose as design (6). The vertical elements also give more lateral area for sailing to windward and somewhat better directional stability.

Deck

There are also many different deck designs. A cambered deck, for example, improves the longitudinal stiffness. One should also make sure that the feet rest comfortably.

19

1

2

3

4

5

6

7 Bottom Shapes

Scoop, Rocker and Volume

The problem of volume distribution is similar to that of outline. A lot of volume and therefore weight towards the bow makes the board more sluggish. The narrower stern used in conjunction with this can be useful.

Little volume towards the bow makes the board more sensitive and restless. A thicker stern allows crossing foaming breakers where the water is less dense and buoyant, and will not sink so quickly in lulls in the wind. Scoop is the upward curve of the bow, rocker that of the stern. Scoop prevents the board from digging in, but too much has a braking effect. A board will not start planing so early when there is too much curve in the scoop line.

Rocker gives more manoeuvrability and better control in turns before the wind. It brakes, however, in turns when the wind is abeam. Boards without rocker are very quick here: there is a lot of lift in the stern and one can press down on this with all one's weight.

A smooth and harmonious design is important. Sharp turns and kinks in the lines (apart from wings and tucked-under edges) almost always bring considerable disadvantages.

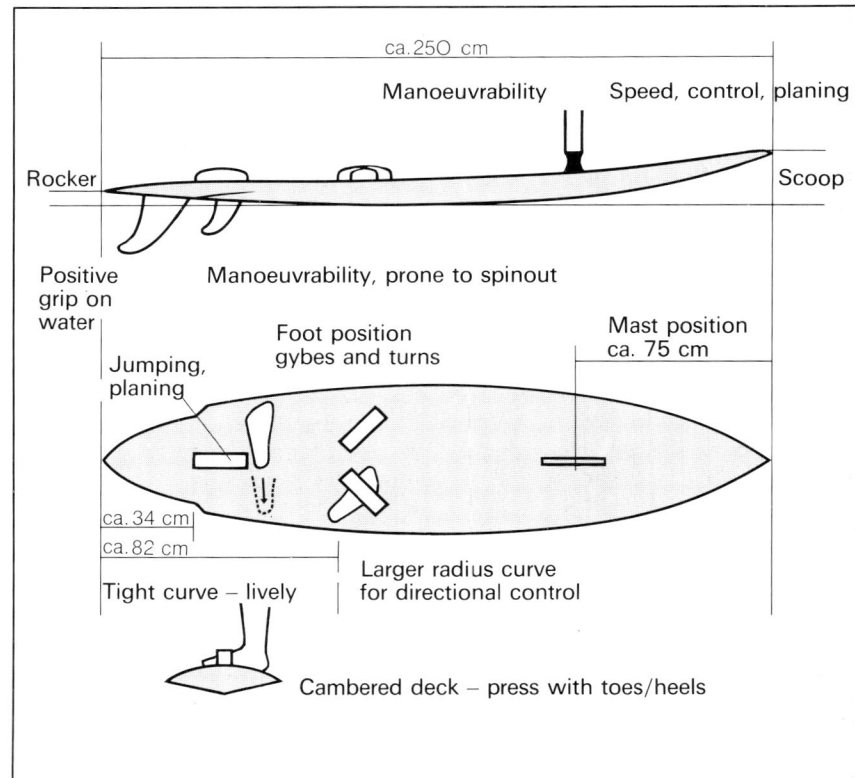

BOARD EQUIPMENT

The Centreboard or Daggerboard

On all-round funboards these are up to 65 cm long and completely retractable. Since they also should not protrude above the deck when retracted they have to be fairly narrow (about 12–15 cm). The resulting small area compared to normal all-round boards and the low lateral resistance must be compensated by a shape that is efficient for speed and lift. This can permit good upwind performance.

The parameters for judging a centreboard are, as for a skeg, the area, profile, sweepback, ratio, length, thickness, stiffness and surface roughness (see page 59).

Skegs

There are a wide variety of skegs or fins on the market in different sizes and shapes. Not every design has received sufficient attention to its functional qualities, or practical testing. Sometimes skegs are used to compensate for poor board design (for example the kanga cock for earlier boards with a lot of volume towards the stern, or football skegs) regardless of the resulting loss of speed.

The skeg area is decisive for the lateral stability of a board, for example after a jump. If the area is insufficient the board will slide away sideways.

The skeg shape determines among other things the speed potential of a board, and also decides at what board speed and angle ventilation and spin-out occur. Flexibility also affects performance.

To prevent injuries, smooth off all sharp or uneven edges.

Skeg Arrangement

Depending on the intended use, the total skeg area is distributed over one or more fins. All-round funboards are usually sailed with only one skeg which is quite long and of fairly large area. The profile should be designed for 20 per cent upwind sailing, 80 per cent broad-reaching and beam-reaching.

Short boards now usually have three skegs, in the so-called thruster arrangement, which normally consists of a large central fin at the back and two smaller side-fins forward of it. The turning axis is on the rear fin, the front fins give stability in sailing curves. A second type of thruster arrangement consists of three fins of equal size. The turning axis is then in the area of the front two fins; the rear fin cushions the turning movement of the board and thus reduces excessive sensitivity.

A recent development in skeg arrangement uses four fins. The two

Thruster arrangement on one of Jürgen's boards. Vee in the tail sections prevents ventilation and thus spinouts. The toed-in outer fins reduce speed somewhat but make the board 'loose' (manoeuvrable)

at the front are larger, the rear pair smaller and nearer to the centreline. This combination is used in low swell. The position of all four skegs toed-in towards the centreline reduces the board's speed and gives a considerable increase in manoeuvrability. Rail-to-rail transitions are safely held by the outside fin pairs. To many people the speed reduction will appear to be a disadvantage. In low swell it is an advantage, however, as it allows the sailor to remain in the wave system without difficulty and to avoid sailing into the wave in front. The combination is useless in calm water, however.

The above comments also apply to all arrangements with angled skegs or those with asymmetrical shapes. The board loses a lot of speed and has a sensitive reaction to foot-steering. In calm water this is certainly a disadvantage, though not in a swell as apart from huge waves one has enough speed from the waves anyway and needs the best possible manoeuvrability.

Footstraps

The closer one comes to slalom sailing and the more one uses foot

Pintail with single fin. This fin has a relatively long chord, which reduces the possibility of spinouts. Long fin box allows fore-and-aft adjustment to alter board trim.

rather than rig steering, the more important footstraps become. They allow exact steering and at high speed and in choppy water they prevent one's feet from being washed off the board. Not to forget high jumps, which are impossible without footstraps.

Good footstraps must meet the following requirements:

—They must stand up even when wet so that one can easily slip the toes into them.

—They must at the same time be soft enough to stand on, and to avoid chafe on the skin.

—They must be light in weight and not soak up much water.

—They must be easily adjustable in height and must not be ripped off in jumping.

—They must offer just enough room for the foot so that the toes stick out on the other side.

—Their position must allow a relaxed stance and be suited to the board's

steering characteristics.

—There should only be as many straps on the board as are really necessary: perhaps 10 straps on a racing board and three or four on a sinker.

Mast leash

The leash or safety line is an indispensable piece of equipment for all boards with any type of release system in the mast step, and should always be attached. On boards where the mast cannot come out under any conditions it is of course unnecessary.

However, fittings do break, and the leash prevents your board blowing away from the waterlogged rig. High wind sailing and surf increase the strains on all of the equipment, and it is better to have a safety leash than to see your 'liferaft' blowing away faster than you can swim after it. Use a strong line and fasten it to the bow of the board.

Mast Step Systems

Certain aspects of the Darby rig are now being revived: on new boards with fin cases for the mast foot fitting the power joint or universal joint is replaced by a system joining board and rig which has a strong similarity to that system. The downhaul line runs through a hole in a plate through the fin case with a knot below the plate. It then runs through a tube about 5 cm long and then through the eye in the tack of the sail to tension the luff in the normal way. The advantage of this system over others lies in its simplicity, allowing for example the early recognition of damage to the universal joint. It is also the system which puts the least strain on the board when jumping. Very stiff rubber power joints or universal joints could drive the mast step through the board or break the board in a hard landing after a high jump.

The above system can of course

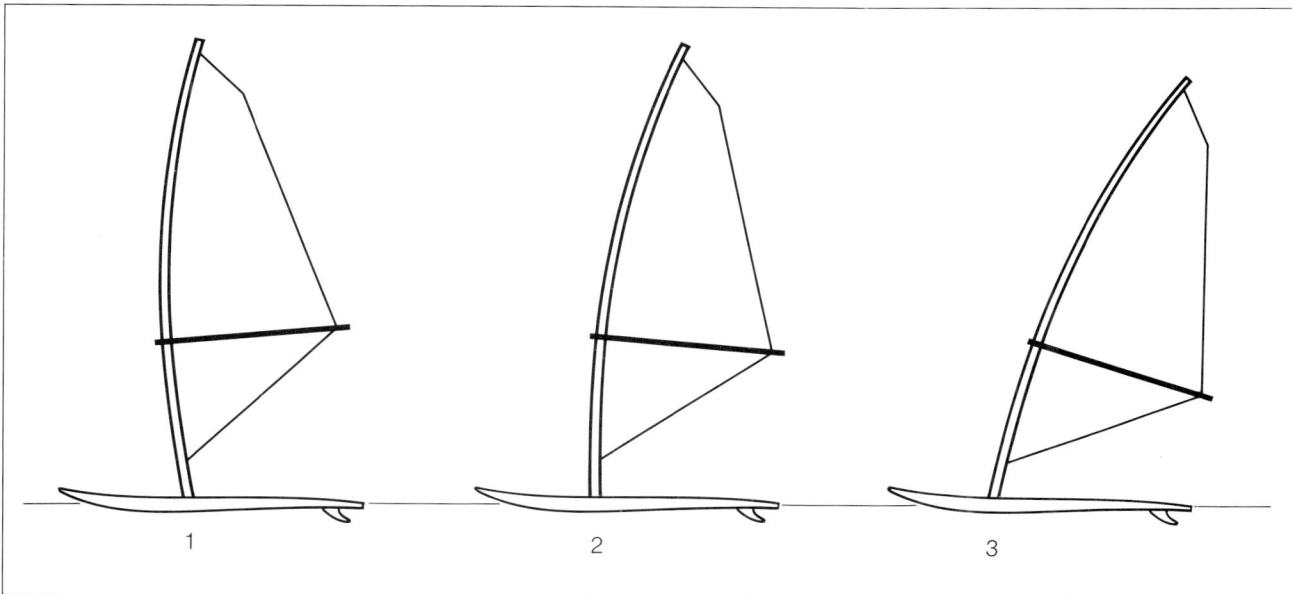

Different rig angles (rake) for sailing in a straight line when the mast foot is at different positions on the track.

only be used on boards where the rig does not pop out, as should be the case on all boards up to 3 m long.

The Mast Track
On all windsurfers apart from those meant for breakers, it should be possible to trim the rig and board according to the conditions using different mast foot positions. For this purpose the mast is on a track.

Ken trying out his wing mast for speed trials. Some features of the curved winger rig are that the battens slope down and the trapeze lines comes down from the mast (not allowed after 1984, however). The wide wing mast has an airfoil section. (See also page 101.)

Sails

The choice of the right sail is just as important as the choice of board to correspond to personal skill and the conditions. To be properly equipped a funboard needs at least four sails. With a difference in size of about 0.5 sq m between one and the next, you are prepared for almost all wind conditions:

Wind	Area	Mast	Boom
Force 8	3.2 m²	4 m	165 cm
Force 7	4.0	4.45	165
Force 6	4.5	4.45	185
Force 4	5.0	4.6	185
below 4	5.7	4.6	210

These figures can vary according to such factors as the sailor's weight and skill, the character of the sailing area and the degree of difficulty of the breakers.

Requirements for High-performance Sails

A modern competitive sail has the following characteristics:
—a high clew, to prevent it dragging in the water.
—a high standard of finish; this includes clean and smooth-running stitches, with extra reinforcement layers and double stitching at the clew, foot and head.
—good quality material (good Mylar or hard-finish woven sailcloth).
—trimming straps on the clew and tack of the sail, for easier tensioning when setting it.
—large, correctly positioned windows that are high enough and extend far enough back; there must be enough height to allow a good view to leeward even with the rig leaned far back.
—battens to stiffen the leech of the sail (unbreakable battens, and fasteners for the batten pockets

which stop them from coming out under any conditions).
—a boom cutout of sufficient width and length.
—layout for a short boom (maximum 2.1 m for a 5.7 sq m sail, 1.85 m and shorter for 5.0 sq m and smaller).
—a good profile and a cut which allows setting to be adjusted between flat and full.
—the widths of the cloths arranged so that they can best bear the tension which arises in that particular area (combination cut). This gives a strong sail without shape distortion.

Full versus Flat Sails

The advantages of a fullness are:
—quickly reaches maximum speed and achieves very high speeds, especially on the wind.
—for the same power as a flat sail of considerably greater area, the full sail is smaller and gives better handling.

Fuller sails can therefore be recommended for calm waters and for coastal areas with onshore winds and wind-induced waves.

In a high swell independent of the wind and with a sideshore wind, larger flat sails are used. Here speed is primarily produced in riding down from the wave crests. Therefore the requirements for the sail are:
—low resistance and hindrance in cutbacks and bottom turns: the sail should be flat to cut through the air without producing power or drag, since gravity is giving the board speed in addition to that produced by the wind.
—a large area. Since wind is very gusty in a high swell (e.g. Hookipa) and there is often not enough wind in the wave troughs, the sail area must be large. This also

applies where water starts are necessary. Here it is the size rather than the curvature of the sail which is decisive.

Racing Sails

As stated above, sails for rough waters only have a slight curvature, with the fullest point fairly far forward. Racing sails, with the clew somewhat higher, are fuller with the deepest point farther back for better upwind qualities (in extreme cases, in the middle). The mast sleeve is wider in order to ensure a smoother airflow from the mast onto the sail by reducing turbulence behind the mast. The mast becomes more difficult to pull out of the water, however, because of the greater weight of water in the sleeve: an opening at the head can help it to drain. A set of sails should ideally have the same luff curvature. Racing sails are used with stiff masts. Sails for breakers get their stiffness from increased tension on the leech via the outhaul.

To cover all possible conditions a set of racing sails should also include four or five different sizes, which could be approximately as follows:

sq m	4.2	4.8	5.45	6.1	6.8
luff	415 cm	430	445	460	475
leech	326	348	365	381	396
foot	206	217	229	243	259
boom	185	200	215	230	245

Mast and Boom

The mast must suit the sail if the latter is to develop the best possible power. In racing the rigs must be as stiff as possible. Aluminium, or for the better-off carbon fibre reinforced masts, are the best for this.

The most common places for a mast to break are around the boom attachment and at the lower end. Here strengthening is absolutely

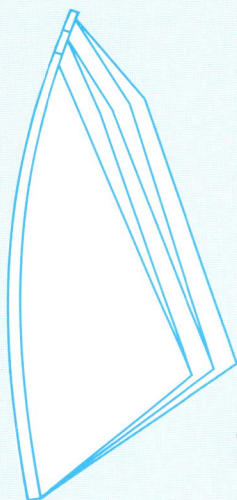

Five different sail areas on three boom sizes. One batten or none.

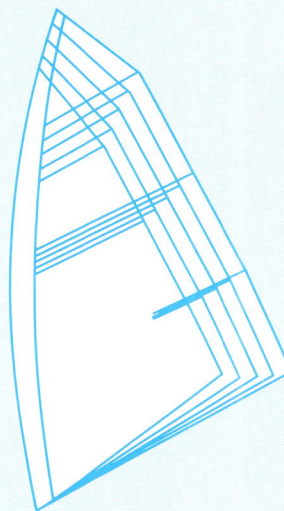

Three-batten racing sails in five sizes. Each needs its own boom.

necessary. In two-piece masts look for a smooth bend when under tension. Around the joint the curve can become a straight line, which you will see causing creases in the sail which cannot be trimmed out.

In 1983 the first profiled masts were used in speed trials, called 'wing masts' because of their airfoil shape.

Sharply bent aluminium masts are, like broken fibreglass masts, usually irreparable.

The boom also has a considerable effect on the characteristics of the sail. It must be wide enough to avoid contact with the fullness of the sail, but not too wide otherwise one's body will be lying flat over the water while the sail is still vertical. This is, however, a desirable quality for speed trials!

Considerable stiffness is most important, and results from the use of hard aluminium tube and hard joints.

A 'soft' boom turns surfing in high winds into a rodeo ride. Every time a wave hits you it bends apart, which shortens the length. This reduces the effective chord length and tension of the sail which then bellies, and to make matters worse the sail's pressure point shifts. The length of the boom must exactly match the sail. If it is too long it is difficult to pull out of the water, and because the clew can move vertically it has the same effect as if it were too soft.

Stiffness must not be at the cost of substantial extra weight. A heavy boom, especially when an extension concentrates its weight towards the clew end, develops huge forces in sail manoeuvres through its high torque and disturbing leverage effects, which will ruin the handling even of an otherwise perfect rig.

The cleats for the outhaul line should be mounted near the aft joint. They are no longer mounted near the sailor's arms for the following reasons:
—it is difficult to readjust outhaul tension while afloat
—the duck-gybe requires a free grip area almost up to the end of the boom
—the holes drilled for the jam cleats are potential weak points, where the boom can easily break if they are mounted towards the middle.

OTHER EQUIPMENT

Mast Padding
When the rig is lying in the water, or thrown around in breakers, the mast presses down on the top of the board. If this is not covered the area where it often lies will be crushed or dented. In order to avoid this equip your mast with a padded protective sleeve such as those in the photos.

Warm Clothing
There are two main categories:
—wetsuits
—drysuits and 'dry wetsuits'.
Wetsuits are normally worn at temperatures over 15°C (60°F) as at every fall fresh water runs through the suit and refreshes the whole body. They must be cut full enough at the shoulders and around the arms to not restrict the blood circulation. Around the body they should fit closely, particularly around the kidneys.

In cold winds you will notice how uncomfortable it is to have seams which are not quite tight and let the wind through. They must all be sealed airtight and watertight. For sailing in breakers one-piece suits are recommended. If you do use a two-piece suit either wear the jacket under the long-john or find another means such as a crotch flap to stop it turning inside out over the arms and torso when you receive a good wash from a wave.

Below 15°C you should use a drysuit. The name is rather an exaggeration, but a drysuit greatly reduces the quantity of water that can enter. There is, however, a certain wetness and condensation inside. As far as I know no-one has yet found a system which seals absolutely tight at the arms, legs and neck when air is pressed out in a fall. One could use

longer and tighter cuffs, but this would make the greatest problem of the drysuit even worse: the circulation to the arms and legs is already so affected that you have to accept a loss of strength. This is the main reason that you should use your wetsuit instead of the drysuit when the water temperature makes it at all possible. Of the two types of drysuit, the plastic or fabric ones made of Arilastic, Goretex, P.V.C., etc under which warm underclothing is worn, and the full-cut neoprene suits, the first type is not suitable for use in the breakers.

The Trapeze
Despite many different ideas and developments, the Hawaii-style trapeze has prevailed over the years. With several additions to the old type it is the most effective piece of equipment for conserving one's strength when windsurfing.

The requirements of a good trapeze are:
—A wide, softly padded back which is anatomically shaped and reaches as far down as the loins. It must distribute the load over the whole back, and should give as little flotation as possible in the water.
—A wide spreader to prevent the chest being squeezed by the straps.
—A tapered hook or a short, relatively open hook (slightly sharper than a right angle) which will release the trapeze line in a fall.
—Quick-release buckles in order to get out of the harness fast if you are tangled up, or to release the tension on the trapeze line if you are thrown onto the sail.

A 'breeches' trapeze like a dinghy sailor's is very comfortable for racing.

It allows the body free movement in all directions and also the suspension and pressure works exactly at its centre of gravity, freeing the back muscles from much of their work. The lower hooking-on point also gives excellent leverage. For windsurfing in breakers it is unfortunately less suitable, because you cannot unhook quite as quickly as with a Hawaii trapeze. The rubber holding the hook at chest level must first contract before the line falls out. There are situations in the breakers which require lightning-fast release, so there it is better to stick to the good old Hawaii trapeze.

Board and Mast Covers
Have you noticed? After a long drive, or when your board has been on the car roof for some time, it is smooth and slippery. The anti-slip seems to be gone altogether. Rubbing with the feet will allow you to stand firmly again and you can also rub the board down first with sand.

It is better to put the board in an overall cover if it is to stay on the car roof for a long time, in order to protect it from being covered with oil, dust and dirt from the road. A thin cloth cover is quite sufficient. If you are travelling by air the cover must be padded in certain places, with specially thick padding over the rails and the edges of the bow and stern. Some jet-set surfers and frequent flyers, however, recommend that you should not pack custom-made boards at all, and thus ensure careful handling by airport personnel. Labelling such as 'Glass – Fragile – Do Not Drop' is helpful, and some sort of wrapping will help prevent scratches and superficial damage and dirt.

If you leave your sail on the mast you must use a mast cover for car transport, as the road dirt attacks the coating on the sailcloth. This will at best ruin the appearance of your sail and these marks can seldom be removed. The cover also shields the sailcloth from ultraviolet light, which will cause it to deteriorate, especially where the sail is coloured.

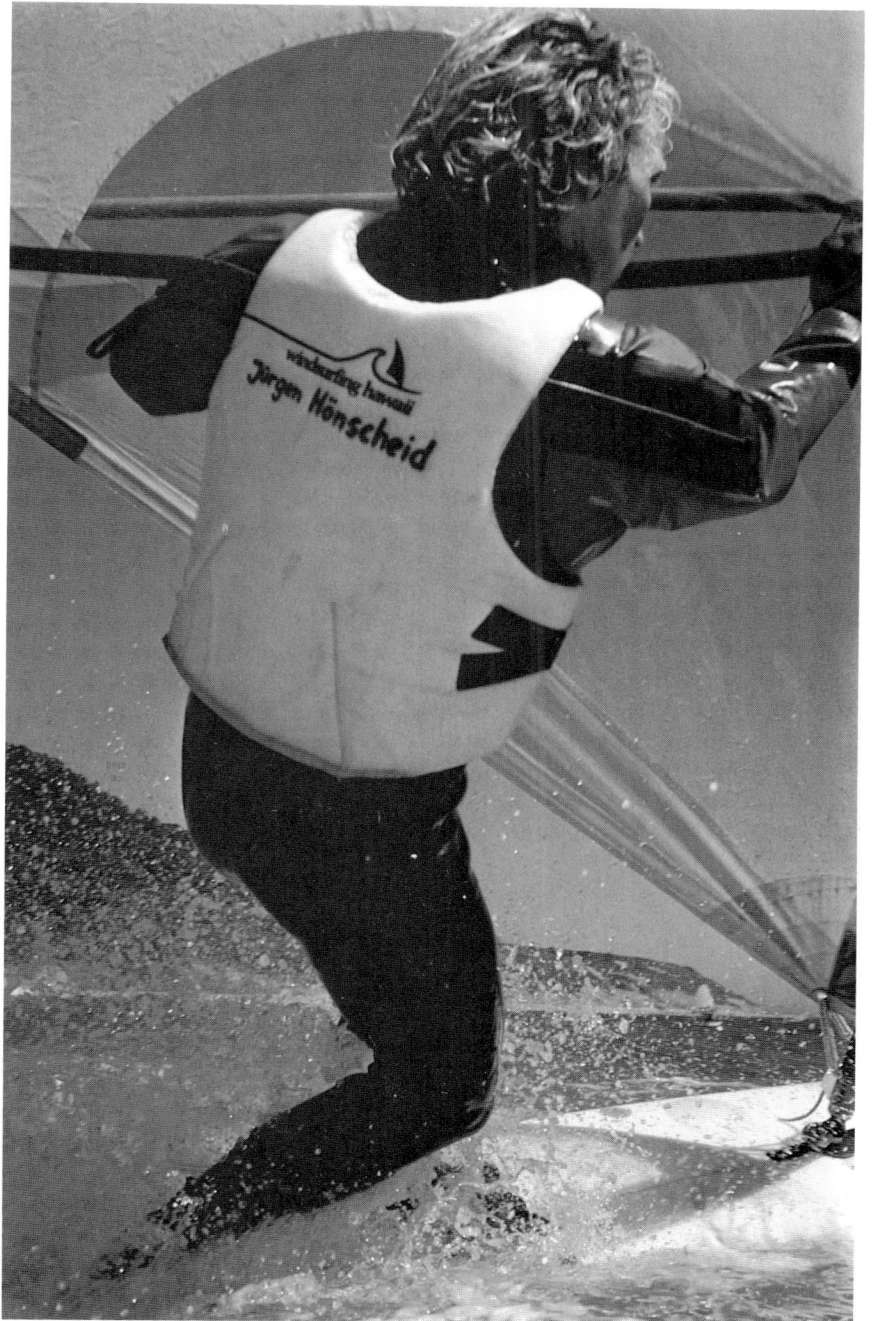

Jürgen at Waddell Beach near San Francisco. The water temperature rarely gets above 60°F (15°C) and a drysuit is recommended.

Wind, Sea and Safety

Getting the greatest enjoyment out of heavy weather windsurfing entails, first, finding rough conditions and, second, knowing whether you can handle them with a reasonable degree of safety.

Windsurfing's dependence on the weather is a mixed blessing: for most people it means hours of waiting and days of frustration at the lack of wind and waves, but it also means unparalled exhilaration when the wind finally does blow and the swell picks up. You should know a little about the wind and where it's most likely to be.

WIND

Wind is generated by various atmospheric conditions and is greatly affected by the land geography. It is a highly localized phenomenon – wind can be 10 knots in one place (not enough for your new sinker), but 18 knots just a mile away (plenty for an afternoon of jumping and gybing) – so the more you know about the wind, the more good sailing you'll have. Unfortunately wind is much too complex to discuss here except very briefly, so if you're interested in a thorough treatment of the subject read *Wind and Strategy* by Stuart Walker (W. W. Norton Inc., New York) or *Meteorology at Sea* by Ray Sanderson (Stanford Maritime Ltd, London).

Gradient Winds

The term refers to wind generated by air flowing from surface high-pressure weather systems to surface low-pressure weather systems; i.e. across a pressure gradient. Gradient winds normally change strength and direction fairly quickly. So if the wind is good you should get on the water and have your fun immediately. Another consequence of changeable winds is that you can easily be caught far from shore by a sudden shift or change in strength. If you're on a sinker, a drop in wind strength can be as bad as a large increase. So always bear in mind that gradient winds are especially difficult to predict.

Trade Winds

These arise from the flow of air towards the Equator direction from the semi-permanent high-pressure cells centered over the oceans in the mid-latitudes. Coriolis effect deflects the flow clockwise so that the trades are nearly easterly in the Northern Hemisphere (westerly in the Southern). The trades are known to everyone as the perfect wind: in our imaginations they blow warmly over tropical waters at just the right strength to make every day windsurf-

Extreme windsurfing requires a good harness: one that distributes the wind's force over the whole back and is well cushioned with buoyant non-absorbant foam which still allows freedom of movement.

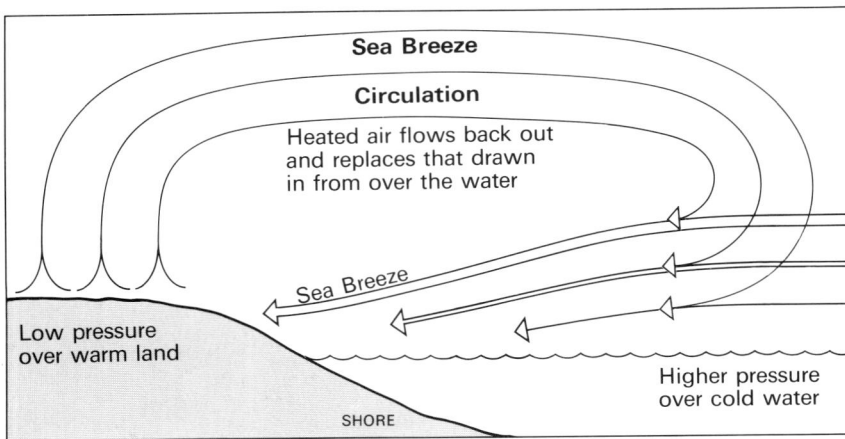

Sea Breeze

Circulation

Heated air flows back out and replaces that drawn in from over the water

Sea Breeze

Low pressure over warm land

Higher pressure over cold water

SHORE

ing perfection. In fact they are remarkably constant in direction and strength, but not nearly as reliable as we tend to believe. They can be absent for weeks, or they can blow very hard. Weather changes relatively slowly in the tropics, so good wind as well as calm will tend to persist for at least a few days.

The highs that feed the trades are larger, more persistent and farther from the Equator in summer, and faster-moving and stronger in winter. So an island like Oahu may get consistent light to moderate trades in summer, but storms from all directions in winter.

Thermal Winds

Generally small in geographic scale and daily cycle, they result when adjacent areas have a great difference in temperature. The hot land causes rising air and lower surface pressure over it while the cool area supplies descending air and a higher surface pressure. Air then flows from the high to the low pressure areas, i.e. from the cooler to the warmer region. The sea breeze is a well known example.

The development of the breeze begins when the sun starts heating

up the land in the morning: the warm land heats the air over it. As the sun's rays become more direct and heat the land more, the air in turn becomes hotter and eventually begins to rise. Of course it doesn't just rise and leave a void near the ground – cool, dense, heavy air from over the sea blows in. This cool air becomes heated in turn and also rises, making way for yet more cool air from offshore. The result is usually a breeze blowing onshore, generally light in the morning, building gradually through the day and peaking in the late after-

noon. Most sea breezes don't exceed 12–18 knots regularly, but fortunately a few do.

Another type of thermal wind is the 'valley wind' such as that on Lake Garda, Italy. It also depends on the sun heating the land, but the area of low temperature is not supplied primarily by water. At Garda the wind blows down the valley in the morning, then reverses at mid-day and blows up the valley in the afternoon. This is because the sun heats the broad plain south of the valley early in the morning, well before it shines on the valley's steep walls. The warmed air from the plain rises straight up and cool air from the valley flows in to replace it, thus generating the morning northerly. At mid-morning the sun finally begins to heat the valley and thus the air near it. As the valley air gets hotter it reverses its previous flow and starts blowing north up the valley toward the mountains.

Local temperature differences alone are seldom sufficient to cause really strong winds. The best thermal winds are always augmented by other factors.

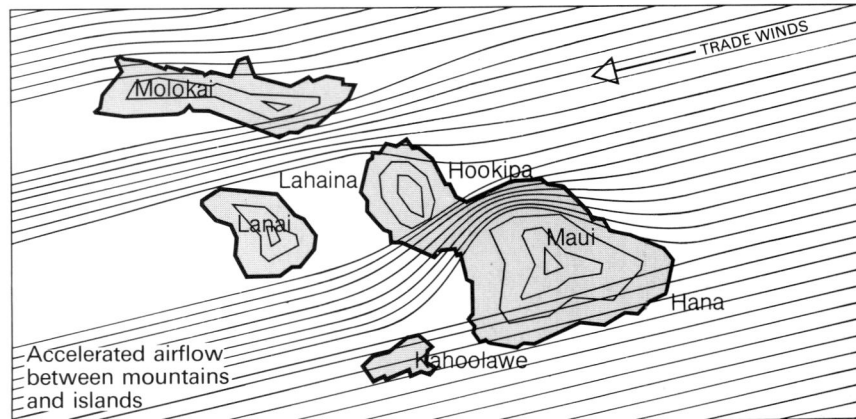

TRADE WINDS

Molokai

Lahaina

Hookipa

Lanai

Maui

Hana

Kahoolawe

Accelerated airflow between mountains and islands

Orographic Effects

Land topography can affect wind in remarkable ways. An example is the effect the Hawaiian Islands have on their trade winds. After blowing unimpeded for hundreds of miles, the trades suddenly meet a chain of high mountains. The wind is forced to channel over, around and between the mountains, and due to the Venturi effect at a much increased velocity. So while filmstars in Hana on the windward side of Maui are playing tennis in a cooling breeze, and the Lahaina tourists are sweltering in the calm of the leeward side, windsurfers at Hookipa are getting upsidedown with 45s and sinkers.

Thermal Mixing

This force is not widely understood or even recognized by sailors. In short, the heating up of the land can do more than just create a thermal wind: it can also increase the velocity of air that happens to flow over it. As the land cools at night the air over it tends to stratify; vertical circulation diminishes and there is no air mixing near the ground. Even though there may be a brisk breeze at 200 or 500 ft air at ground level may be dead calm. As the land heats up during the day and pockets of warmed air start rising, the fast-moving air from aloft is forced down to the ground in strong gusts. So regardless of whether there is a thermal wind in your area, the wind will still tend to be strongest in the afternoon.

Combined Effects

Most places known for good strong winds benefit from topographic and thermal effects that augment the prevailing gradient wind. A good example is Waddell Beach in northern California which has a NW gradient wind that combines on summer afternoons with a NW sea breeze. The coast has some bends to the north so that the breeze must flow over warm land before reaching Waddell. Furthermore, inland from Waddell is a small range of mountains. It is likely that a gradient wind, thermal wind, thermal mixing and Venturi effect all combine to create the exceptional (typically 20–30 knot) summer winds that prevail at Waddell Beach.

Another example is Buzzards Bay in Massachusetts. The SW gradient wind of summer is reinforced by the southerly sea breeze. This then flows across the Elizabeth Islands south of the bay and is further reinforced by thermal mixing. An afternoon wind of 20 knots is common on Buzzards Bay.

Sea Conditions

While wind is very important to windsurfing, it is its effect on water that makes the sport most exciting. The ups and downs, ramps, holes and moving terrain of the windswept oceans give sailors an unparalleled variety of thrills and challenges.

Waves and Swell

For as long as the local wind blows the resulting waves are referred to as *sea*. Such waves are characterized by steep, irregular faces and short wave lengths. On a protected body of water where the waves are small and short the term *chop* is often used. when the wind ceases, however, the waves become less steep and lower though they continue travelling across the ocean until they reach a shore on which to break. Waves no longer generated by wind are called *swell*.

The racing sailor usually does not have to pay much attention to swell, but must handle rough seas. The surfing sailor prefers to jump and surf the waves from a swell, but can have fun in breaking seas also. Swell is surfed in places like Hawaii, California and the West Country in England – though any exposed coast can also experience swell. Seas are surfed in places like Holland, Sylt and the south coast of England.

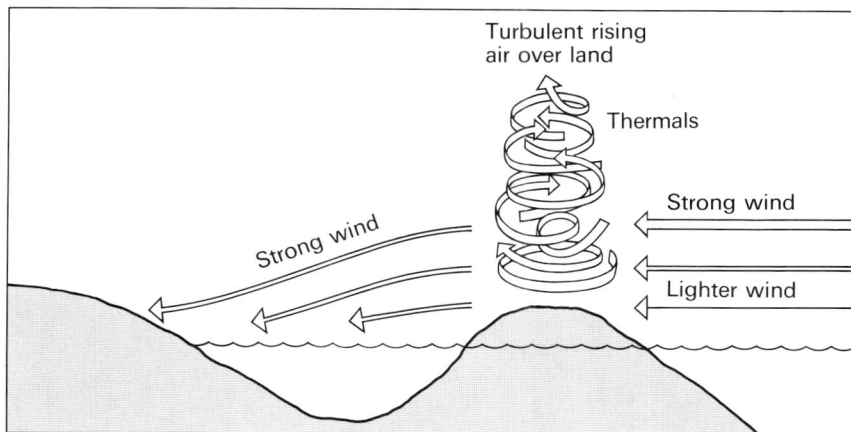

Turbulent rising air over land

Thermals

Strong wind

Strong wind

Lighter wind

Strong wind

Surf

Waves break in three ways, one of which we won't discuss because it is of no use to windsurfers.

Rollers

Rollers form as waves break over a bottom which becomes shallower gradually. A roller becomes gradually steeper as it nears the shore, until finally the top quarter or third of the wave tumbles or spills forward. It will continue to break in this relatively innocuous fashion until it reaches either the beach or deeper water. Rollers are called *mushy waves* and are the best ones on which to become acquainted with the surf.

Plungers

Waves which break over a rapidly shoaling bottom form a high peak quickly and then break from top to bottom in a violent fashion. A plunger converts nearly all of its potential energy into downward kinetic energy at the moment it breaks, and is therefore most dangerous then. Perversely, or perhaps predictably, top surf sailors seek to get as near as possible to the point of greatest danger and kinetic energy.

There are three more effects that the sea bottom can have on a wave: they are illustrated on page 34.

Refraction

A wave approaching a straight beach at an angle will tend to bend so that when it breaks its front is nearly parallel with the shore. Surfers call this tendency *wrapping* and find it useful in several ways. If a swell originated to the NW, for example, the beaches directly facing NW will receive the biggest waves. A beach nearby which faces SW will receive the same waves reduced somewhat

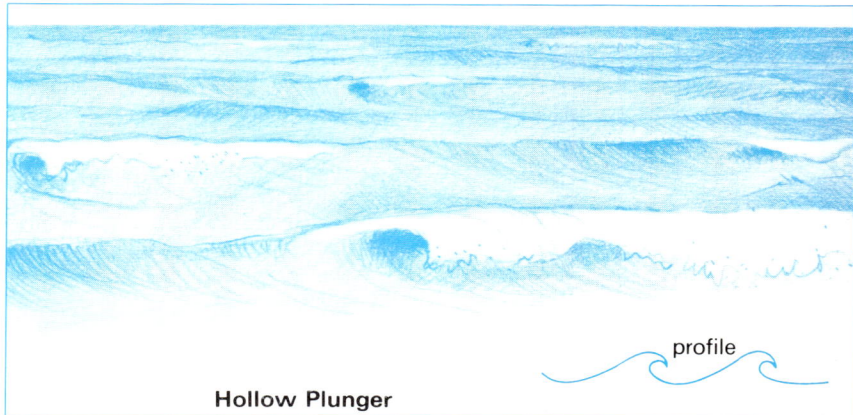

profile

Wind Waves

profile

Mushy Roller

profile

Hollow Plunger

Above: something of the power contained in a hollow breaking wave is shown here. Even a much smaller wave has the force to throw a windsurfer and break his equipment.

Opposite: wind-driven waves form 'white horses' or 'whitecaps' as the wind strengthens, and break heavily in gale conditions. However, they are more randomly spaced and do not form the continuous, evenly spaced lines that are typical of breakers on a shore or reef.

Side View of Swell

Peak

Trough

in size and increased in wavelength by the fact that they had to refract around a point or bulge of land. The refraction effect also occurs around islands, and sometimes shoals.

Convergence

If there is an underwater ridge perpendicular to the beach the portion of the wave directly over it will tend to break first, thus creating a peak from which the surfer can go either right or left. The alluvial fan of sediment dropped by streams as they join the sea is an example of an underwater ridge which creates a peak. The good thing about a ridge is that it can cause the waves to break in nearly the same place every time.

Divergence

A submarine valley perpendicular to the shore has an opposite effect. The part of the wave over the valley will tend to break late or not at all. Valleys can create channels through the surf, so that one can get out through the waves without encountering any white water at all. They are especially helpful when the surf is over mast high. Waimea Bay on the north shore of Oahu has such a valley. Only the largest waves break there.

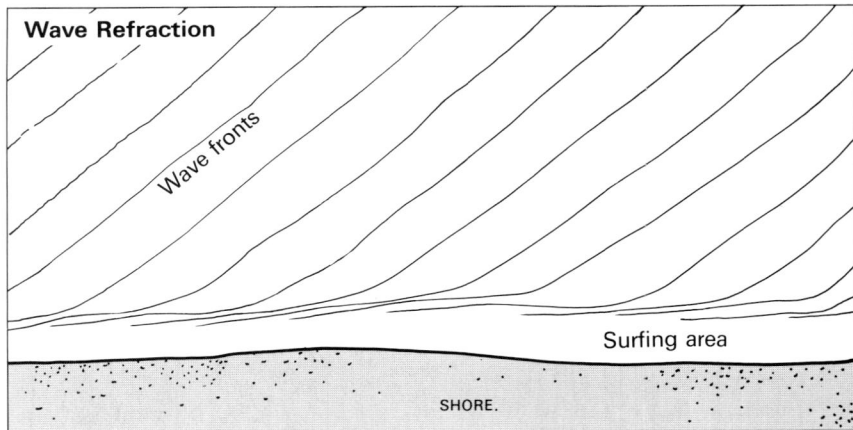

Wave Refraction

Wave fronts

Surfing area

SHORE.

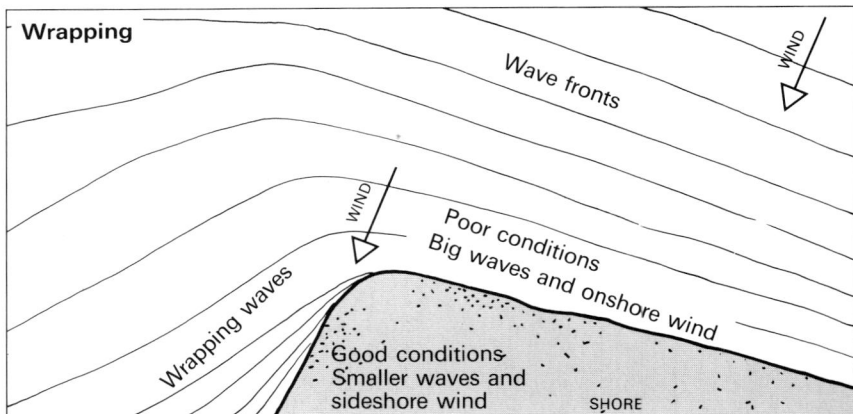

Wrapping

Wave fronts

WIND

WIND

Wrapping waves

Poor conditions
Big waves and onshore wind

Good conditions
Smaller waves and sideshore wind

SHORE

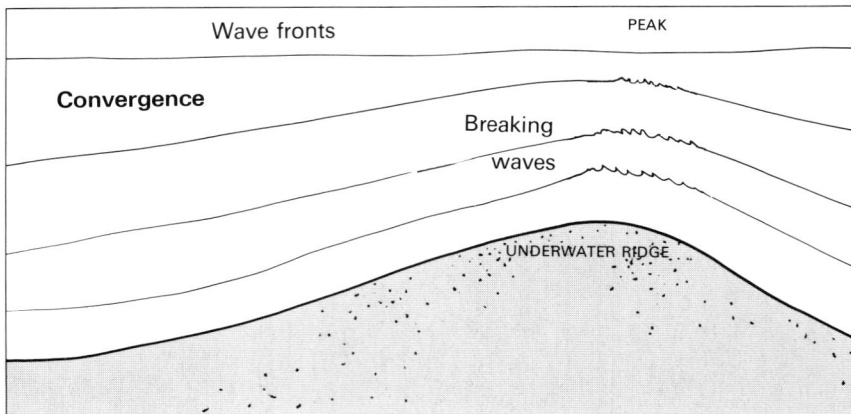

Wave fronts

PEAK

Convergence

Breaking

waves

UNDERWATER RIDGE

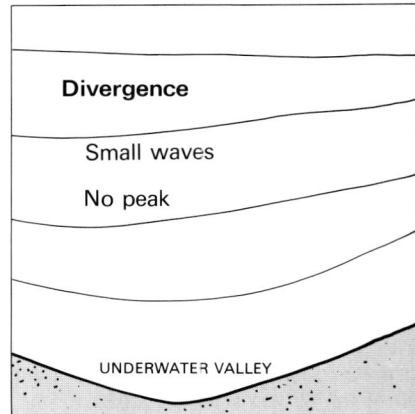

Divergence

Small waves

No peak

UNDERWATER VALLEY

Currents

Currents can have a profound effect on sea and sailing conditions. For example, in the entrance to San Francisco Bay the tidal current flows west through the Golden Gate during the ebb and east during the flood. When this stream, which can exceed 5 knots, flows (ebbs) against the 20–30 knot westerly sea breeze, it does the following:

—Carries small boardsailors upwind so they can bear away and sail fast all the time.

—A 5 knot current into the wind increases the apparent wind by 5 knots. Thus wind which would be only 20 knots to an anchored boat appears to be almost 25 knots to someone sailing into it.

—Wind against tide causes large, steep, choppy waves, providing good jumping.

—Thermal mixing, enhanced by the warm bay water, increases the surface wind strength.

When the tidal current flows with the westerly wind (floods), these effects are reversed. It's difficult or impossible to stay upwind on a board that doesn't have a centreboard, the water is flat, the wind is moderate and it tends to come to the surface only in streaks and patches.

Currents are not always obvious, but they can be found everywhere. Off the North Sea beaches of Holland and Belgium, for example, the tide flows alternately one way then the other. Since good winds blow from the SW quite often there, many wave sailors prefer it when the current is flowing toward the SW, giving steeper waves.

Strictly speaking, currents can be caused by either tides, in which case they are also called 'tidal streams' and change direction at regular intervals, or by prevailing winds which may change direction or strength with the seasons but tend to be steady for long periods.

You must know the geography, wind patterns, and tidal streams in your own area in order to use them to enhance your sport.

The tidal stream (current) in San Francisco Bay, as in many other places, strongly influences sailing conditions.

Safety

High-performance windsurfing has its rewards and its risks: the most exciting conditions are sometimes the most dangerous. Thus it is essential, both for the good of the sport and for the good of the sailors, that everyone knows the risks and how to mitigate them.

That isn't to imply that windsurfing is a dangerous sport the way car racing and hang-gliding are dangerous. In fact it has a remarkable safety record, but still it's possible to suffer cuts and bruises and much more serious injuries if proper caution is not used.

Ever since the late 1960s there has been heated debate over whether windsurfers should be required to wear personal flotation devices (PFDs), otherwise known as buoyancy aids or lifejackets depending on their construction. In some countries they are required, in others not.

It's amazing, though, to experienced windsurfers that so much debate is centred around the subject of lifejackets when in fact the subject of safety is very broad. PFD use is but a small part of this large topic, and to pay exclusive attention to PFDs is like a team of surgeons clipping the toenails of a heart patient: there are more important matters to attend to.

Hypothermia

This condition, of lowered deep body temperature, is arguably the most likely and the greatest danger the average windsurfer faces.

Some people aren't willing to spend money on wetsuits, so they lack adequate protection from cold. Weakness, fatigue and poor balance and judgement can result, and the sailor may find himself unable to get back to shore. Children, who are the

least likely to know about the danger of hypothermia, are the least likely to be able to afford a wetsuit and also, because of their low body mass, the most vulnerable to hypothermia. They also tend to stay on the water too long, heedless of shivering and fatigue.

A day that seems warm on the beach can be very cool on the water, especially when a strong offshore wind is blowing. An ill-clad sailor can quickly become fatigued and unable to sail, and consequently drift out to sea. This can happen even without falling in. A person who has just bought a new sinker might be able to sail it well enough to get wet and cold, but not well enough to get back.

The wetsuit that feels toasty and warm while you're sailing hard will feel icy cold while you're sitting on your board ruefully contemplating a

One of the most radical mano-euvres, that surfboarders could only dream of: 'off the lip'.

broken universal joint. If there is a chance that you could be stuck out on the water without adequate protection, don't go. If you find yourself shivering and shaking uncontrollably, immediately find a source of heat and warm yourself thoroughly. If you wait too long it may be very difficult or impossible to reverse the cooling on your own.

Losing the Board

On well built and maintained boards it's nearly impossible for the rig to become accidentally separated from the board. The mast foot will pop out on most production boards, but there is usually a safety leash that ties the two loosely together. This link is vital, because it prevents the board from drifting away after a fall. The board is the sailor's liferaft, and without the sea-anchor drag of the rig it can blow away too fast to catch by swimming.

The universal joint can break unexpectedly on a windy day, and the unprepared sailor could fail to catch hold of the board before it drifts away. If your board doesn't have a leash and you're planning to sail farther from shore than you would care to swim, then you should wear a lifejacket.

Don't sail alone, be sure someone knows where you're sailing and when you'll be back, know the weather and your own capabilities.

Separation from Shore

It's common for a beginner to sail away from the beach with no problem but be unable to manage the other tack at all. If he hasn't gone far, it's a simple matter to roll up the sail and paddle back.

An experienced sailor can also find himself in this position. But if he's on a sinker and conditions are rough, paddling in with the rig could be impossible.

—It's cold, it's late, there's no one else around, you're on the ocean, there's a strong offshore wind and your skeg has just broken.

—A cold front just came through and that 20 knot sideshore southwester has suddenly become 30 knots offshore. You're overpowered and can't sail upwind.

What can you do in such situations? You can abandon your rig and try to paddle back on the board while you hope someone on shore misses you and knows where you went sailing.

Problems in Surf

Wave-riding on a sailboard is much like surfing. A sailor in surf is generally within swimming distance from shore, he'll frequently need to swim short distances to recover his board after a fall, and he will dive under breaking waves and surges of white water to avoid their full force. Thus gear that impedes efficient swimming, on the surface or below, can be a hazard. Bulky boots, thick wetsuits, lifejackets and large harnesses do not facilitate swimming (though in some waters the heavy wet or drysuit may be essential for keeping warm enough).

Surf sailors are not likely to be separated from their boards or the shore, but they do have to watch a few other things.

Coral and rock reefs are hard and often sharp. Minimize your contact with them. When you fall into shallow water don't dive, or stick down an arm or leg, but rather land flat like a pancake so you won't go deep and hit the bottom. When you water start, don't kick with your feet until you're sure that doing so won't mean kicking sharp coral or barnacle encrusted rock. If you have to cross a very shallow reef (1 ft deep) don't walk, instead float across on the board by walking your hands gently along the bottom. One further reason to avoid the bottom in tropical waters is that sea urchins are frequently present. Their long spines can stick into your skin even through bootees and cause considerable discomfort.

Your equipment can hurt you more easily in surf than anywhere else. During a bailout in the air or a wipeout in the surf you can be hit in the head or neck with the board or mast, or cut by a skeg. The way to avoid such mishaps is to get well away from your equipment whenever you have a bad crash. If you know on takeoff for a jump that you're out of control, you should bail out early. The wind will then have time to blow the board away from you. If you abandon late, you'll have to keep an eye out for the board to make sure it doesn't land on you or vice-versa. If you're surfing a wave and wipe out, dive away from the board, roll up into a foetal position and put your arms around your head. When you come up for air don't lead with your face; you don't know what's up there, so precede your face to the surface with one hand. That way, if the next surge of white water is carrying with it someone else's board your hand, not your face, will absorb the impact.

Always be aware that breaking waves are very powerful. If a surge is pushing a board or rig in your direction, move. Also, to make your equipment less likely to injure you and others, your boards should have rounded tips (nose, tail, wings, etc.) and you should round off the edges of your skegs with sandpaper.

Currents are found where there is surf. Breaking waves carry water toward the shore and *rip currents* carry it back out to sea. Typically there is a *longshore current* parallel to the beach, and a rip current perpendicular to it. Longshore currents are most common along straight beaches and are caused by waves

Look out for wave-born pieces of equipment. Protect your head with your hands while coming up after a bailout, to avoid colliding with a board or a rig like this.

approaching the beach at an angle. They are usually no more than a nuisance: staying upwind is difficult, and getting started again after a fall can be especially hard. The rip current, on the other hand, is less innocuous since it is travelling away from the shore. If you find yourself separated from your board and in the grip of a rip, don't try to swim toward shore. Instead, swim parallel with the shore and you will soon be out of the current. You can then body-surf the waves in to the beach.

Waves When you're swimming after your board you can easily see that breaking waves can be powerful and dangerous. Even waves only head high can be surprisingly powerful if they are hollow. So always know when a wave is about to break on you so that you can dive under it. The bigger and hollower the wave, the deeper you have to dive under it and the harder you should swim. If you don't dive deep enough the wave can catch you up in its circulation and tumble you around until you're very nearly out of air.

Other people and their equipment are a very real hazard of wave-riding. Collisions and falls have caused some very serious injuries, and surfboarders may be sharing the same breakers as sailors. Before your first sail in a strange country or sailing area, find someone knowledgeable to explain to you all the local rules about who has right of way and where you should be sailing. The following usually apply.
—Look all around you before gybing or turning.
—Surfers are less manoeuvrable, so they have right of way over boardsailors. (They are also harder to see.)
—A person riding a wave towards shore has right of way over someone going out.
—The person nearest the breaking part of a wave, or riding the wave that is farthest out from shore, has right of way.

Off long straight beaches the current often runs parallel to the shore (longshore) and turns back out to sea where it meets an opposite longshore current: this can cause a strong rip.

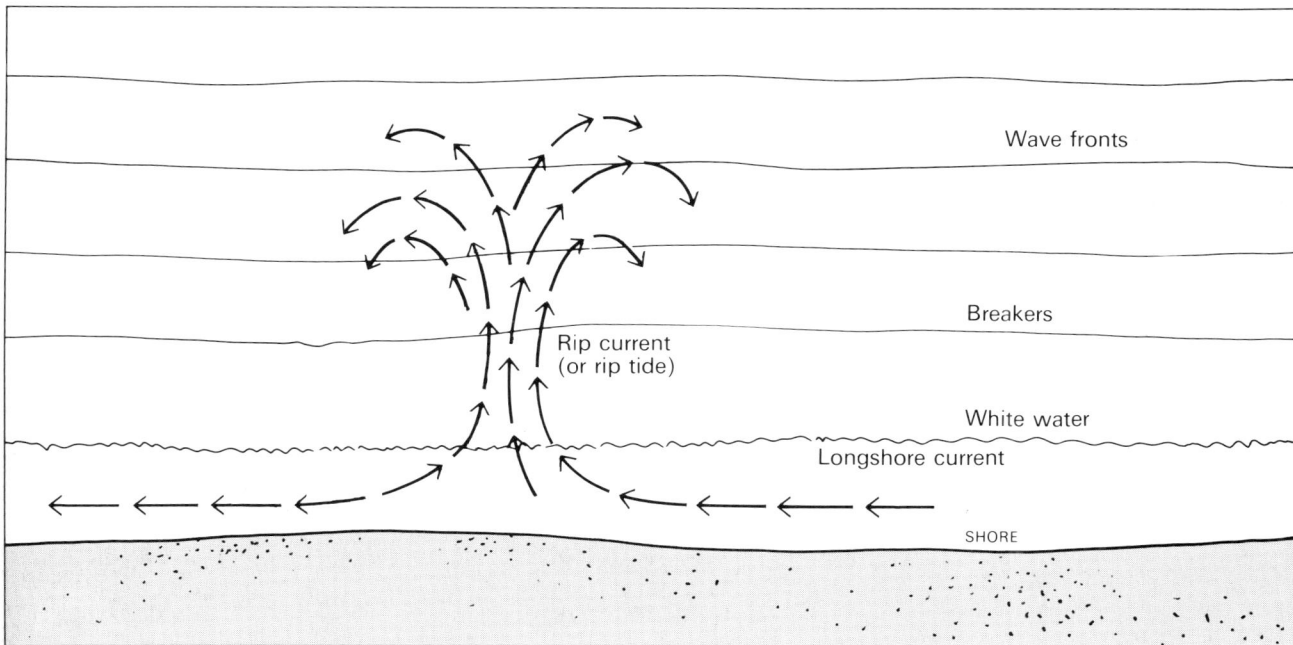

Wave fronts

Breakers

Rip current (or rip tide)

White water

Longshore current

SHORE

Funboard Techniques

When you read the following chapters perfecting your technique on funboards you will already have the basic steps of windsurfing behind you. You will be able to master the basic manoeuvres on long boards with the centreboard down, so that you can easily sail off in any direction in winds up to Force 4. You can steer with the rig and feet on the outer rail and carry out emergency stops, tacking and gybing safely and smoothly with only 10 per cent error – in ten manoeuvres in Force 4 one at the most goes wrong. Now you can go on to funboards. In an earlier chapter we have already described the boards best suited to the different levels of ability. Now we will describe the skills which you must learn at each level in order to work up towards becoming an expert windsurfer.

BASIC TECHNIQUES
A: all-round sailors

You must now learn to steer the board by controlling it with the feet. This is only possible with a retractable daggerboard. The steering techniques with a daggerboard down which you have already learned are completely reversed, so you must

relearn in terms of the changed behaviour of the board: starts (in strong winds, beach start), foot-steering, tacking, gybing (power gybe), sailing stance and trapeze technique.

It is best to learn on an all-round funboard. As an all-round (A) sailor you will be able to enjoy all the manoeuvres under almost any conditions on a board of this type.

Starts

The strong-wind start is, in principle, the same as the basic start:
—The feet are placed at a distance behind the mast.
—The rig is angled by rotating the body forward, turning to face more towards the bow.
—The sail hand is placed on the boom, then the mast hand grips the boom.
—The sail is hauled tight by rotating the torso back, so the trailing shoulder is turned towards the stern.
Before going out in very high winds, try starting with the board in positions other than with the wind abeam. It will then no longer be necessary when starting to carefully turn the board so that the wind is abeam.

When getting under way in strong

winds there are many problems which make it necessary to vary the above basic routine:

—Strong winds produce choppy waves, which when the board is positioned across the wind will strike it directly on the side and considerably disturb the balance.

—The greater wind pressure on the sail demands the use of body weight. The sailor must push himself out of balance to windward in order to balance against the wind pressure.

—The considerable acceleration of the board shifts the relative wind forward at lightning speed and demands fast and extensive sheeting-in while using body weight to balance at the same time.

—The tendency of the board to turn into the wind, if the rig is not leaned enough to windward, can lead to its turning into the wind too quickly for control to be maintained.

The following starting technique will help deal with these problems:

Karsten Kemmer doing a perfect start on an all-round funboard. Above: aligning the board at an angle to the wind and waves. Opposite: aligning the rig, positioning the hands, sheeting in by turning back the body and leaning it to windward. After the start, bearing away on course. Sail position is adjusted by the back leg.

—Point the board with the bow at an angle to the waves (in an onshore wind, closehauled).

—Go far back behind the mast; you may put the front foot into the rear strap.

—Pull the rig over at an angle to windward so that it is slightly overweighted to windward.

—Place your hands on the boom a shoulder-width apart.

—Straighten the forward leg and push the body backwards.

—Haul in the sail by straightening the backward leg; push the body to windward and turn it back in order to do so.

—Change course to the desired direction.

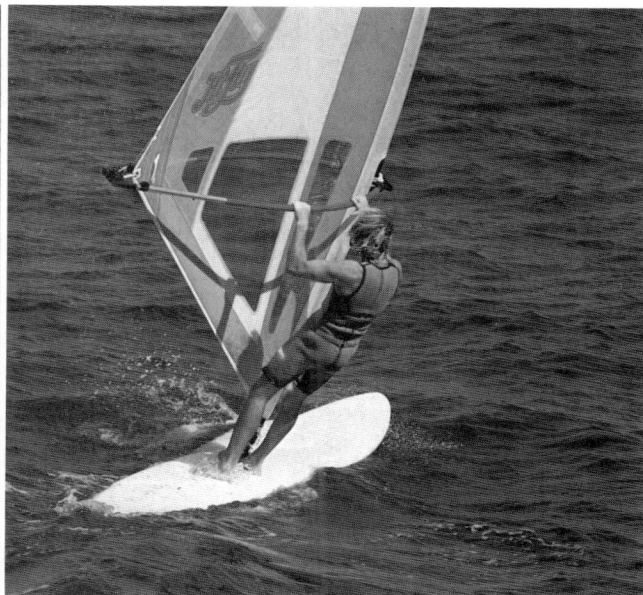

On boards with the daggerboard retracted you can stop the board luffing up by stretching out the feet (with the centreboard down, by putting weight on the heels).

Ken in a high-wind position with his weight to windward.

The Beach Start
This is useful in so many ways that you cannot do without it. The rig and board are already connected for a beach start and the rig is held up while entering the water. Balance difficulties caused by the waves can be prevented from the start because you don't first have to haul the sail up out of the water. There is less strain on equipment, especially the rig, as this does not have to drift separately and out of your control while you fetch the board.

Beach starts have a lot in common with water starts and can therefore be a considerable step in this direction (a beach start with the water deeper than the hips has more in common with a water than with a beach start). There are four phases:
—preparing the rig
—entering the water
—pointing the board
—getting on and starting to sail.

Entering the water

In order to get the board and rig into the correct relative position, go with the mast in front of you to windward and stand beside the stern. From now on only the mast hand holds the mast; the other points the board and later controls the sail position.

The clew of the sail should be downwind of you and the mast.

In order to slide the board into the water tip it onto the leeward edge. You can do this by lifting it holding one of the skegs on the windward side (inadvisable in heavy seas as there is the danger of cutting yourself) or a windward footstrap, or you can hold it flat against your body.

Now you can push the leeward bow edge into the water, always holding it at right angles to the water coming into the shore. If you want to bear away hold the board flatter; to luff up increase the angle. When the water is deep enough for the skegs, lay the board flat. This is the basic entry technique, which is particularly suited to long boards. It is important that the board enters the water on edge, since if it is pushed in flat it will easily dive or be pushed under by the waves.

Small boards up to 3 m long can be carried into the water. This avoids wear and tear on the board as it does not have to be pulled through the sand. You may also be able to walk out through the waves breaking directly on the shore. In order to carry the board without wasting strength, you can lay the sail on your head. The rig then counterbalances and lifts the board. The pivot is your head. Alternatively, hold the mast foot and board pointing into the wind with the rig laid flat. The wind will then get under the sail and board and support them. This method requires a lot of experience, as the angle to the wind must be constantly adjusted, otherwise the board will shoot upwards or the wind will press from above and drive the bow to the ground.

In both methods the board is guided by the sail arm. It is held by the side footstrap with the lower arm laid over the board.

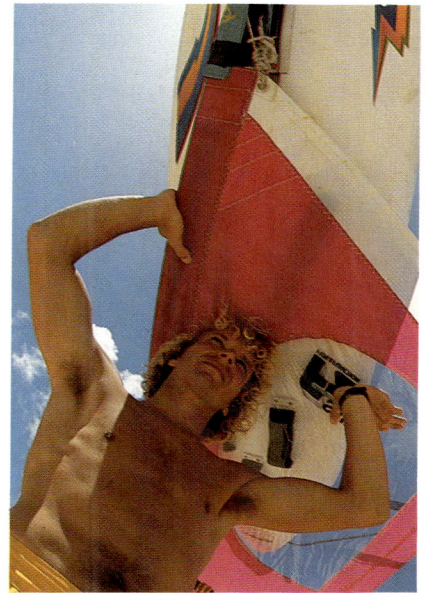

Some ways of carrying the board to the water. The board and rig can be balanced against the wind, or with the sail on one's head (left). Let the clew end of the sail 'fly' downwind. Sail and board can both be carried on the head (above).

Pointing the board
In rough water the incoming waves will knock the board off course. This must be promptly corrected. When the board is flat on the water the mast and sail hands must immediately grip the boom in order to steer more effectively.

To luff up:
—increase the angle of the board while you are still carrying the stern
—step to leeward, if the stern is still raised
—lean the rig to leeward.

To bear away:
—decrease the angle of the board, if the stern is still raised
—step to windward, if the stern is still lifted up
—lateral pressure on the mast.
At all times before the actual start the board must be at a right angle to larger waves and any breaking ones, or it will be washed away. You can only keep control if you stand near the stern: any farther forward and the board will turn away out of control.

Getting aboard
Before getting on push the board into knee-deep water. First point the board so the wind is abeam, then place your back leg on the board and pull it towards you, so that the board is turned onto a reaching course. With this pull the rig is upright and can develop more power. You complete the beach start by hauling the sail tight and at the same time pushing off the ground. When you climb onto the board with your other leg the stern will normally sink a little under the pressure and the board luff up slightly. You can reduce this or balance it out on a board without a centreboard by putting some pressure on the leeward edge.

The less static lift there is in the stern of your board the farther downwind you must point before getting aboard, as otherwise it will sink under you.

Below: beach start into waves. Use the 'smooth' between two sets to get underway very quickly, trying to pick up as much speed as possible while sailing towards the oncoming waves.

Pages 46 and 47: you will have to balance the board against the waves. If the shore break is very strong, carry the board over it and then put it down. Another way to get past the shore break is tail-first.

Foot Steering

Boards with the daggerboard fully retracted react above all to foot-steering. Weight on the leeward rail makes the board bear away, weighting the windward rail makes it round up into the wind. If you only want to make a slight change of direction both feet can remain in their straps. You then bear away by stretching out the back foot or pushing the rear knee forward and to leeward. To luff up pull the back foot up sharply (pressing with the heel) and put more weight on the front foot.

For sharper changes of course the back foot must be taken out of its strap. To bear away it is moved to leeward and weighted with knee pressure, supported by the front foot pulling up the board by the strap. For wide-radius curves the back foot should be placed somewhat farther forward, in front of the strap. For radical course changes, turning almost on the spot, the foot is farther back.

To luff up the back foot is moved to windward and pressed down. This movement above all requires practice. It is difficult to luff up sharply and nevertheless make the board turn smoothly. For practice we recommend slalom courses with the wind abeam. Start with a slight curve, with the feet in the straps. Then take out the back foot and sail large-radius curves with your weight moved forward. Finally, sail curves with your weight back, and radical changes of

Bearing away and luffing on a funboard, clearly showing how the knees are pushed out to leeward and slightly forwards (above). This gives a wide carved turn. The sail is slightly luffed (below) to help turning up into the wind.

direction covering an angle of at least 90° from your course with the wind abeam.

You should never forget that although steering with the rails is the essential element on a funboard, rig steering also has a part to play. To bear away the rig is moved to windward as before. To luff up it is moved to leeward.

If you steer far enough to upwind and downwind of your course with the wind abeam you will very quickly reach the point where the sail must change sides in order to be on the correct side in relation to the wind. As you already know, on bearing away you must gybe, on luffing up you must tack.

The Gybe

The gybe is the preferred manoeuvre in windsurfing. Whereas tacking is accepted as a necessary evil, the gybe is a harmonious part of quick and elegant funboard sailing.

Funboards
On boards without a daggerboard there are two types of gybe:
—the power gybe (shifting the sail over the bow)
—the duck gybe (shifting the sail clew-first over the stern), described in the next section on Advanced Techniques.

The two main gybe techniques. Above: Jürgen swings the sail over by holding the mast. Below: he pulls the foot up and over his head to shift the sail across in a duck-gybe.

Basic Forms of Power Gybe

A prerequisite for gybing is mastering foot-steering. Before starting the move you must look out to leeward, in order to make sure that you will not hinder or even collide with anybody.

The individual stages are:
—Stretch the back foot out and to leeward.
—Weight the back foot and pull up on the front foot.
—As you then bear away off the wind, carefully let out the sail (it must always be filled).
—Bear away past the dead downwind heading. After the stern passes through the wind the mast tilts backwards and the boom end points forward so you are sailing with the clew forward.
—Change foot positions while turning through the wind: the back foot goes forward into the sidestrap, the front one comes backwards.

1

2

49

—The sail hand grips the mast, so that the sail turns to leeward and pulls the rig somewhat to windward. At this point the mast hand releases the boom.

—The former mast hand grips the boom on the new side and hauls the sail tight.

—After briefly letting out the sail so the new mast hand can shift to the boom, you get under way on the new heading.

Tips

The greater the speed of the board and the tighter the turn, the more you will have to lean into the curve.

The sail must be filled at all times during the gybe. The loss of speed caused by a flogging sail which has been let out too quickly leads to the stern sinking and the slipstream breaking off the skeg, so that the manoeuvre can only be completed with difficulty if at all.

In starting a gybe you can haul the sail a little too far towards the stern, in order to bear away more quickly. It must then, however, move forward with your body weight for better control of the board.

The radius of the curve in a gybe is governed by the position of your back foot and the distribution of your weight on the board. The same rule applies as for steering: the farther forward your weight, the wider and more precise the curve; the farther back, the tighter the radius and the less controlled the turn. (An extreme case is the pivot gybe, turning on the stern, described below.)

The forward hand grips the mast before shifting.

Variations

Apart from the one-handed and pivot gybes described later on, variations

concentrate on different grip changes and timing of the foot shifts.

Grip changes

The technique described above is in our opinion the surest one. You are, however, free to shift hands like Kai Schnellbacher, for example. He grips the mast with the mast hand before starting to bear away, and controls the rig during the turn with the mast and boom.

I only move the mast hand towards the mast before bearing away. When I shift, the sail hand changes grip at once from one side of the boom to the other. I don't use the mast at all.

Footwork timing

In front of a wave, you often shift the sail before changing your foot position, and only move the feet once the sail is already on the other tack. You shift the sail over earlier than in other power gybes.

Ken's gybe (below, right to left). Bearing away by pushing with the knees and leaning inward (1), the rig tilted to windward. Despite leaning into the turn, the clew is slightly forward (2). After shifting over the sail, changing foot positions (3–5).

5

4

Jürgen's gybe (above, from right). Bearing away by pushing the knees inwards and a little forward, into a widely carved turn (1). Because a wave is coming up behind he tightens the turn by leaning back, so he is at 90° to the breaking wave after gybing the sail (3–5). Once past the surge of white water he starts again (5).

Right: again bearing away for a widely carved gybe. The back leg is bent and pushed well down. The rig is raked to windward despite the sailor leaning into the turn.

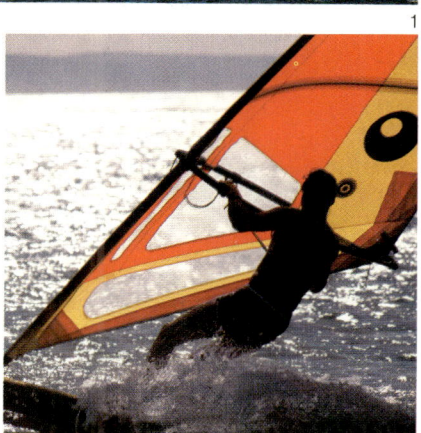

Tacking

If you are going to tack without a daggerboard you should first take up a position farther forward. The stages in going about are: luffing up, grip and side change when into the wind, and the start on the new tack (sometimes bearing away offwind).

Luffing up

In most conditions you can round up so far into the wind that the sail is already slightly on the new tack (backed slightly). To luff up, weight the windward rail, let out the sail a little and tilt the rig to windward. In the resulting curve haul the sail in tight, parallel with the direction of movement. From the point where you are on the wind stretch out your mast arm with the mast hand on the mast. Also place your front foot just ahead of the mast.

Changing sides

To change the sail over take weight off your back foot and move it directly beside the front one. The sail hand now takes over the mast. After half a turn of the feet, one foot goes back into a strap on the new upwind side and the mast is pushed far forward at an angle.

Moving off on the new tack

The sail hand is now on the other side of the boom and the sail is hauled in tight. In sheeting in the front foot goes behind the mast and the back foot puts light pressure on the lee rail. While letting out briefly the mast hand is moved from the mast to the boom.

Variations

It is possible to vary the timing of the tack and the grip changes: in strong winds you luff up only as far as the eye of the wind. It is also possible to luff up and sail through the eye of the wind with both hands still on the boom. When you step in front of the mast the sail hand then grips the mast.

In strong winds it is sometimes better to grip the mast with both hands while changing tacks, and then to throw it to windward. Both hands then change grip to the other side of the boom.

Many sailors hook up the trapeze line while hauling in the boom on the new tack, and do not then have to let out the sail to place the mast hand on the boom.

Sailing Position

The best possible stance is most important for saving energy and for safe, fast sailing. You should only start using a trapeze on the basis of a good sailing position. This includes the angle of the sail in relation to both the wind and water, and your position on the board.

Positioning the sail

On all courses, except before the wind, the propulsive force of the sail is caused by lift. By setting the sail chord at an angle of 15°–20° to the relative wind striking the sail's cross-section a force is developed which operates like a pressure gradient at an angle forwards and to leeward. It is important to be able to feel exactly the right angle of the sail to the wind, since any other will cost you speed and perhaps energy.

The rule also applies on funboards, that the sail should be sheeted in only so tight that the flapping of the luff just disappears. Since you sail with the relative wind, which is constantly changing its direction and force according to the speed of your board as well as the changes in strength and direction of the true wind, you must constantly check and adjust the sail's position. Especially with the sail trimmed flat and a short boom, it can very quickly be hauled in too tight without your noticing. The airstream from leeward to windward is broken and the sail stalls and only produces very little power, without demanding a greater pull on the boom.

With a boom over 2.10 m long and a fuller sail, the broken airflow also reduces the effective force of the wind. The loss of power is not so great, however, and so this power works almost entirely sideways and cannot be turned into speed. Then you waste strength fighting the sail to keep the board upright rather than using it to sail forwards.

The angling backwards of the rig is also important. It reduces the gap between the sail and the board to a minimum and prevents the pressure on both sides being equalized by flow underneath the sail. If you pull the sail area slightly farther than usual to windward, the angling-back of the rig gives the bow lift and allows the board to start planing early.

Body stance

The correct stance is most important for sailing with the minimum effort. It must be such that the sail is correctly angled and tilted without twisting or bending the body. If your hands are a shoulder-width apart on the boom and equidistant from the sail pressure point, you are standing so that a vertical line down from the pressure point would pass exactly between your feet. The body should be stretched with the torso parallel to the plane of the sail. This is the only way to ensure an equal distribution of effort over the whole body. In light conditions the feet should be a shoulder-width apart, in strong winds farther.

Trapeze Technique

The description of trapeze technique is closely related to the sailing position: there is no such thing as a trapeze technique on its own. The most important aspect of trapeze sailing is preparation:

—Selecting the right trapeze.
—Attaching the trapeze lines with a trapeze knot.
—Correct positioning of the trapeze lines on the boom: a shoulder-width apart with an equal distance on each side of the sail pressure point. After testing this may be adjusted: if the pull is too strong on the mast hand slide the line forward; if it is stronger on the sail hand move the line aft.

If you have mastered the correct sailing position it is no problem to swing the trapeze line into the hook with a quick movement of the boom, in order to keep your arms free for steering and correcting the sail position. To remove the tension from the hook pull the rig in slightly towards you. The saving in energy can tempt you to sail at higher speeds with a trapeze than you could control without it. This can be seen when you have difficulty in getting hooked on to the line and are constantly fighting to balance the sail. This usually ends in a spectacular catapult fall, and often equipment (mast, boom, sail) gets broken. Make it a rule only to sail with a trapeze in those wind speeds which you can hold without it. You should not be hooked in while jumping.

If you fall it is important to hold on tight to the boom with both hands. This applies particularly if you are catapulted off. You thus avoid being injured by the boom, and also avoid the danger that your trapeze line could be wound around the hook as a result of the corkscrew motion in such a fall.

Spinout

There are three types of spinout. The first occurs on boards at high speed with a forward foil (high-wind daggerboard) immersed. It acts as a pivot and lifting surface. Whenever one pushed too hard with his back foot and overloaded the skegs the board would head up sharply, shoot to windward or even try to spin round.

More modern boards that have either a completely retracting dag-gerboard or none can round up or slide sideways very quickly. They won't shoot to windward because they don't have that powerful lifting surface forward.

The third type is more of a slide. Usually on a fast broad reach, the skeg will seem to lose its grip. Nothing violent happens: you just skid like a car on ice.

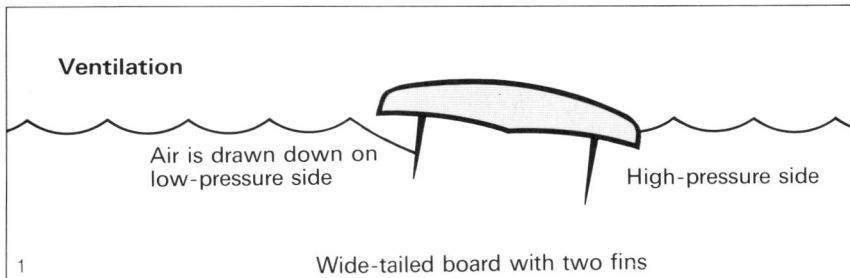

Ventilation

Air is drawn down on low-pressure side

High-pressure side

1   Wide-tailed board with two fins

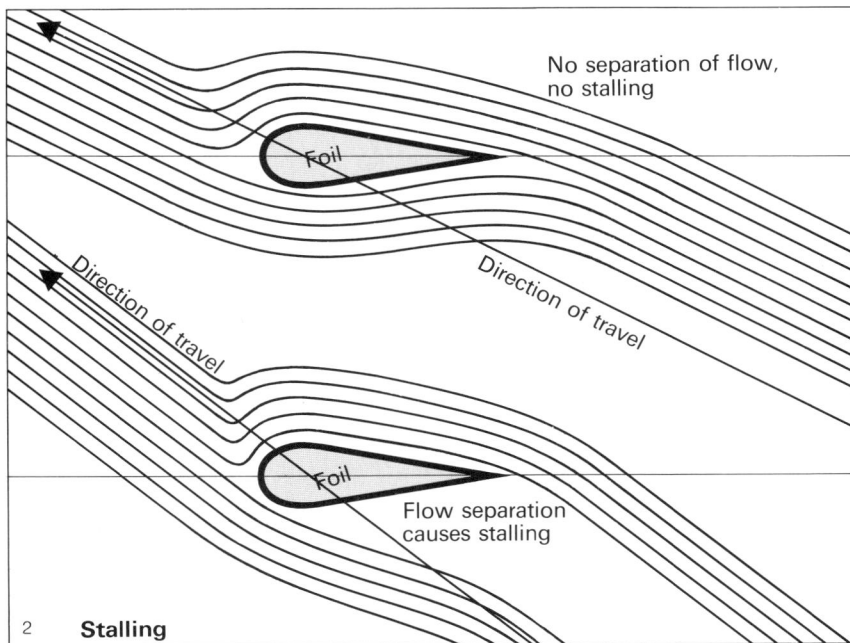

No separation of flow, no stalling

Foil

Direction of travel

Direction of travel

Foil

Flow separation causes stalling

2   **Stalling**

Stalling

If a foil (such as a skeg or rudder) is pushed through the water at too high an angle of attack (too much sideways rather than forward) the water flow on the low-pressure side becomes separated and the foil's lift (in this case lift means resistance to sideways motion) drops drastically. Stall is the culprit in most spinouts.

Ventilation

A foil operating near the water surface can suck surface air down its low-pressure side. Entrained air greatly reduces its effectiveness. It's not uncommon to see the tip of a windward skeg with no water around it: just a hole in the water upwind of it. This is most likely when the fin is near the edge of the board. Ventilation is often the cause of sliding spinouts.

On a twin-fin board, when the windward fin is ventilating madly the leeward one will be making neither sound nor bubbles; the bottom of the board 'insulates' the fin's low-pressure side from the water surface (and it is deeper) so no air is entrained.

Cures

Rigs, boards and skegs all effect the tendency to spinout.

Sails Those with long booms (8–9 ft/2.4–2.7 m) can cause spinout. A gust can shift the centre of effort aft drastically and cause you to have to take a tremendous sudden load with your back arm. But to do so you have to push against the board with your back leg, which can stall the skeg and cause spinout.

This same effect works with old blown-out sails and light woven cloth ones. The draft moves aft in a gust and your reaction overloads the skeg. Tightening your downhaul a lot to pull the sail's draft forward can help control this problem, as can new expensive sails made of Mylar or non-stretch sailcloth.

Masts
Flexible masts let the fullness move aft in a gust and thus contribute to spinout. Use as stiff a mast as you can afford.

Boards
Wide-tailed and flat-bottomed boards are most liable to spinout. Yet such boards are fun: they plane quickly, go fast, have a lot of buoyancy and jump easily. If you've got one and are having spinout problems, put more and bigger fins on it. Three right across the tail is a good arrangement, or if the tail is rounded somewhat the two outside fins can be set forward as thrusters. To reduce ventilation, keep the side fins a couple of inches in from the rail.

Narrow Vee-bottom pintails are the least likely to spinout, even though they usually carry just one moderately sized fin. A bigger fin often works.

For any board between these extremes, spinout can generally be corrected by more or bigger fins. Channel and concave bottoms in my experience are not solutions.

Skegs
Fins have many characteristics that affect performance: sweep, taper ratio, plan, section, aspect radio, tip shape, fillets, thickness, stiffness, surface roughness, chord length and fences.

Sweep forward helps prevent ventilation, but catches anything in the water every time you pass over a bit of kelp. Drastic sweepback is theoretically inefficient, but shifts the

A low jump and bearing away in mid-air helps stop spin-out.

fin area farther behind your back foot. Your leg thus doesn't have as much leverage over the skeg and is less likely to overload it. A slight amount of sweepback, enough to shed weed and fishing lines but not so much as to be inefficient, is probably best.

The profile is the shape from the side. The semi-ellipse is theoretically best, but a trapezoid that approximates the semi-ellipse is considered nearly as good, and is on many World Cup racing boards. Still, plain old surfboard skegs like fish fins seem to work fine on most boards.

The *cross-section* approximates the foil shape seen on plane and bird wings. GRP fins usually have a large flat on each side and ridges of resin near the leading edge. The molded polycarbonate ones are generally unfair, and have ridges at the edges where the two halves of the mold joined. These are faults that should matter, but it's very difficult say how much they do. The first contact with

reef or rock will bring to naught the superior qualities of your ideal fin. Recreational boards receive too much abuse for any great concern for perfection of finish. It is important, however, to round off all sharp edges, for safety.

High *aspect ratio* is the most efficient, but a skeg of too high an aspect ratio is easily broken or can tear the skeg box out. Too deep a skeg can cause the board to want to tip (rail ride) at high speed. Also, a high aspect ratio foil will stall easily and suddenly, especially at low speed. Fins of low aspect ratio are strong and stable, but inefficient and slower in turning. Moderation is best.

Anti-ventilation fences isolate the lower part of the foil and prevent air entrainment. Several such foils seem to be successful.

Thick fins are harder to stall but can have greater drag at speed. Skegs $\frac{1}{4} - \frac{5}{8}$ in. thick have worked well.

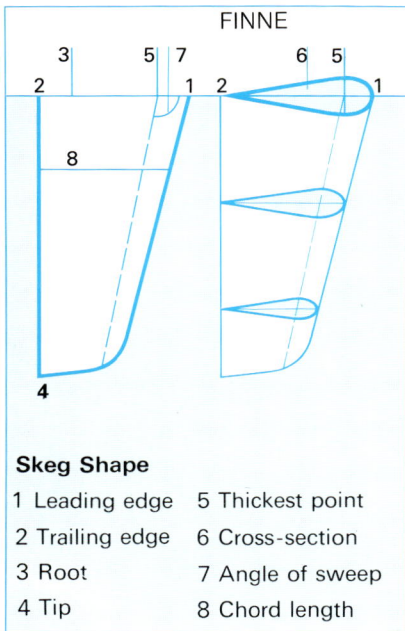

FINNE

Skeg Shape

1 Leading edge	5 Thickest point
2 Trailing edge	6 Cross-section
3 Root	7 Angle of sweep
4 Tip	8 Chord length

Techniques to Prevent Spinout

Try to keep your back foot ahead of the skeg. With pintails this is no problem; on wide sterns have plenty of skeg area. If you feel early painful fatigue in your back thigh bring the forward foot back so your weight is more evenly divided. Hang your weight on the boom, with less on your legs. The board is then driven through the mast, with less chance of shoving too hard on the tail.

In jumping you often head up a little so on landing the board (and skegs) are going sideways and stall; also the wind blows you sideways. To prevent spinout on landing, head off slightly in mid-air. Tilting the weather rail up lets the wind catch the bottom and blow it downwind, rotating it bow-first. As you take off tilt the rig slightly forward and upwind: you may head off too much, or take a nosedive, but it will help you head off.

Correcting a Spinout

For sudden moves, bank the board so the upwind rail digs in and head off by tilting the sail forward and hanging on the boom. This transfers a lot of drive to the mast and forces the bow round.

One way to counter slow skids is to pull the tail to windward with a leg jerk. This momentarily unloads the skeg and may clean up the water flow. Or hop off a little wave, only high enough to get the skeg out, and bear away in mid-air.

ADVANCED SAILING TECHNIQUES
S: sport sailors

The most important aspect at this level is adapting to the slalom-funboard, which has no centreboard at all and reacts mainly to foot steering. The main problem here is not learning new techniques. You must first develop a feeling for the board, as it reacts very sensitively to:
—weight transfers (by sinking the bow or stern or tilting on one side)
—steering movements of the legs (by luffing up or bearing away quickly, or 'flutter', when you are poorly balanced and must constantly adjust the balance with your feet).
A further problem is to find the best angle for your board to sail to windward. Only if you succeed in

this will you be able to enjoy its full potential when reaching. Being able to get to windward is also essential for your safety.

The techniques that you learn at this stage make you more mobile on the water. They are also enjoyable to watch, and give you a lot of experience in manoeuvring your board. Now learn:
—the water start
—the helicopter tack
—the duck gybe
—the pivot gybe.

The Water Start
In high winds the water start is usually the safest and least strenuous way to get your board moving. You do not have to worry about balance. Also it requires less effort to raise the rig from the weather side with the help of the wind than to haul

it up from the leeward side into the wind. On sinkers, simply hauling up the sail is in any case hardly a practical proposition.

The water start has three stages:
—ensuring the correct rig position and lifting the sail out of the water
—pointing the board
—the start itself – getting under way.

Lifting the sail out of the water
The sail can be easily raised out of the water on condition that either: (*a*) the rig lies to windward of the board with the clew towards the stern, *or* (*b*) the rig lies to leeward of the board and the clew points to leeward.

The rig must now be positioned so that the wind can strike the luff at an angle from the top. If the top of the mast is now lifted a little and pushed to windward, the wind will get under the sail and it will be lifted off the water.

Now you haul yourself by swimming with one hand on the mast

Radical duck-gybes, executed by Ken and Jürgen

down to the boom, and shift your hands onto it. If the sail is lying to leeward, swim to the stern and pull the sail with the mast hand low over your head to windward. The sail hand then grips the boom and the mast hand follows at once. Pulling slightly tighter raises the rig a little and offers more area to the wind. This also applies if you swim closer to the board.

If there is not too much water on the sail you can sometimes clear it with a strong swimming stroke. This applies particularly in waves, when a wave has just passed. If a fall to windward is inevitable you should therefore keep your hands on the boom and extend your arms.

If you are lucky, a strong swimming stroke will at once let the wind catch under the sail again and lift it out of the water. If the sail is lying the wrong way round you must swim into the wind with the clew and lift it a little so that the rig turns over. If it is wrongly positioned to leeward it is often worthwhile to lift the sail slightly with the uphaul line and then to fall with the whole rig to windward. Sometimes it is then also possible to keep the rig clear of the water.

If the board and rig have turned so that the water start will not set you off in the right direction, carry out the start anyway in the given direction and then gybe.

Water start when the rig is on the lee side. Jürgen lifts it out of the water and swims it mast-side first round to windward (1, 2), turning the board under it so the wind is abeam (2). The hands grip the boom, the sail is held up in the correct position, the wind striking it at an angle from the top (3).

When the rig is out of the water the back foot is put into its strap. The sail is then already filled.

Directing the board
You can point your board with the following steering movements:
Luffing up
—leaning the rig to leeward
—stretching the back leg sideways.
Bearing away
—sideways pressure on the mast, swimming to leeward
—pulling in the back leg
—pushing down the stern with the back leg and pulling it under the body (only possible if there is little static buoyancy in the stern).
The board is now headed so that the wind is free. The sail position must also be correct for this.

Getting moving
To get under way the rig is held as vertically as possible and the boom pulled in a little tighter, and at the same time the torso is bent forward and you stretch out as far as possible. On boards without a centreboard place light pressure on the leeward edge to counter the luffing up. When the body is out of the water place the front foot on the board in a strap. On sinkers, the stern is pulled under the body and the front foot put into a strap before pulling the sail in tight. In starting, on a course which should be well downwind, the weather edge is pressed down slightly.

The board is turned onto a broad reach once the feet are on it. The upright sail is pulled in while the knees push forwards (4, 5). The board will try to luff up a little (5). After a successful start steer for the next wave (6).

Below, from left: waterstarting in light wind. The mast is held with one hand to get the sail more upright. The lower you grip the mast the higher you can raise it and the less wind you will need to get up.

Above, from right: water start clew forward. After a fall while gybing, try to keep the sail off the water and turn the board onto a broad reach. Haul the sail in by pulling the mast.

The Helicopter Tack

For funboards this is a way of tacking in lighter winds; it can only be sailed in breezes up to Force 5. You would use it, for example, after surfing a wave against the wind, in order to cross the line of breakers once again. On boards with little volume in the bow and the mast set far forward it is the only sensible way to tack (gybing is always better). The manoeuvre incorporates important elements of the 360° turn and can therefore be sailed as a preliminary exercise for this.

The movement sequence:
—Luff up through the wind using combined rig and foot steering.
—Push the rig forward and away from the body: light pressure of the sail hand backs the sail. The weight is laid forward, the rig goes far out towards the bow.
—The pressure on the sail hand is increased until the sail swings over in front of the mast.
—The sail hand grips the mast, the mast hand is released and the sail is hauled to windward.
—The feet move to the new sailing position.
—The former mast hand grips the boom and hauls the sail in tight.
—While letting out briefly, the mast hand moves from the mast to the boom.
—Set off with the wind abeam on the new course.

In this version both hands stay on the boom until the sail changes sides. A further version, not quite as good, is to shift the mast hand to the mast while luffing up and to pass the mast to the sail hand when the sail changes sides. The sequence is otherwise the same as that described above.

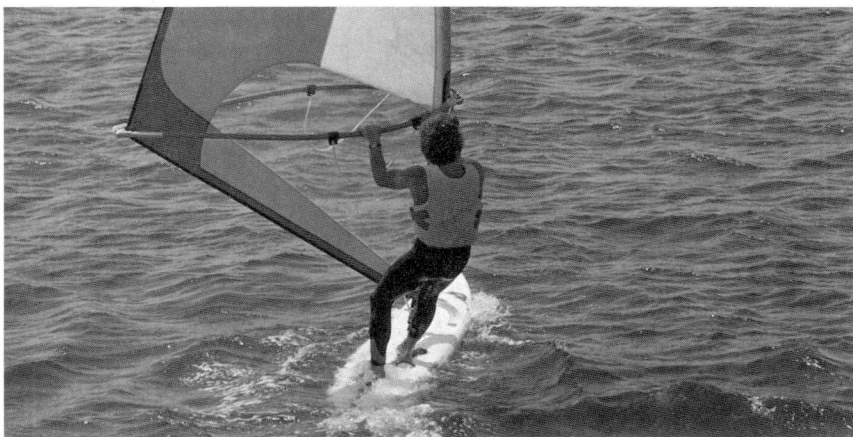

In this manoeuvre timing is most important, especially on small boards: it is better to sail out of a gust before starting a helicopter tack.

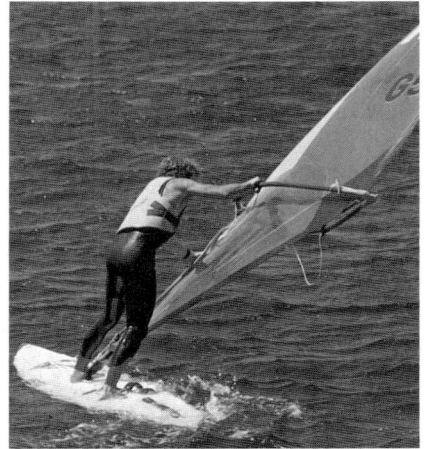

Above: After the board has luffed through the wind and the sail comes back, you must push the rig well over to windward.

Photo sequence: the sinker or helicopter tack. Luffing through the wind (1, 2) and raking the rig well forward and to windward (3). The sail will not be luffed while the board is bearing off on the new tack. Give way to the stronger pressure on the mast and push harder on the boom (4). With the clew forward and the foot positions changed, the sail is ready for shifting over (5). On sinkers the tail will be immersed while you are tacking the sail, so it is essential to get wind in the sail again as soon as possible in order to regain enough dynamic lift.

The Duck Gybe

This gybe, in which the mast instead of the clew is swung across the bow, is a manoeuvre which requires a certain amount of experience on funboards. You must be able to keep the board planing well, to maintain the sensitive balance required throughout the manoeuvre, and always to know where you are heading at a particular moment (i.e. the direction of the true wind). A successful duck gybe is already begun during your approach. You must decide on the point where you will carry it out.

—It is best to make the gybe where the water is as smooth as possible (for example in front of a wave), as you will then be able to maintain board speed as long as possible.
—The higher your speed, the wider radius curve you must sail.
—In choppy water you should sail a tighter turn.
—In a gusty wind make the gybe in a gust. This must not on any account die down while you are turning through the wind.

The movement sequence:
—To start, the back leg is moved sideways to leeward and weighted with the knee bent forward at an angle. This makes the board bear away. This 'inside' position must be maintained through the whole manoeuvre.
—When the wind is over the stern grip the clew end of the boom with the mast hand. The mast swings over the bow.

Left: the necessary speed for a good duck-gybe is easily held in front of a wave. Right: Jürgen and Ken duck-gybing.

—Grip the other side of the boom with the sail hand as far forward as possible, reaching up under the sail at an angle to do so and pulling the rig slightly back.

—Change with grip of the former mast hand and correct your sail position on the new course.

—Change foot positions when three-quarters of the turn has been completed.

Problems

The main problem is for the board to maintain enough speed in the turn to carry you through the whole manoeuvre. To ensure this you must:

—Carry out the manoeuvre in as smooth water as possible, or use the momentum in front of a wave.

—Start the gybe on the fastest possible course with a free wind, and increase speed by pumping.

—Sail a clear-cut gybe with a wide radius. The body weight moves forward at an angle to leeward.

—Haul the rig back carefully when you take hold of the other side of the boom.

For beginners the main problem is to maintain the 'inside' stance. This applies particularly when changing grip to the other side of the boom. Usually they lay back when diving under the rig: this leads to the board luffing up slightly and the sail pushes them backwards into the water. You must therefore:

—As a beginner start the gybe early, before turning dead downwind.

—In gripping with the former sail hand, lean forward at an angle and try to grasp the boom as far forward as possible.

—In hauling back the rig look forward to the former sail hand and haul the rig 'behind you' with the other.

Variations

There are a number of variations of the duck gybe, which usually involve the order of the grip changes. For example, mast hand on the foot of the sail, then change grip to the other side of the boom; or, the mast hand reaches immediately under the sail to grasp the other side of the boom and the sail hand follows. Apart from the last variant, which saves one hold, they are mostly questions of style. For learning, we recommend the form described above.

Below, from right to left: the duck-gybing sequence. Bearing away by pushing down the lee rail: the sail stays closehauled (1). The mast hand crosses over towards the clew end of the boom, the sail hand lets go and you duck under the foot (2). Try to grip the boom on the other side as far forward as possible (3). Finish turning the board after gybing over the sail (4–6).

6   5   4

If you have relatively little speed you can let out the mast early and then haul the rig backwards at an angle with a powerful tug when you reach under the sail. The rig will then stand free for a moment, giving you the chance to grab the other side of the boom with both hands at the same time. In this variant the board comes to a standstill when shifting, and the stern sinks considerably.

3

2

1

Pivot Gybe

This sinker gybe is probably the most radical change of direction in windsurfing (wave-riding apart). The board turns on the spot through an angle of up to about 150°.

The movement sequence:
—Briefly feather the sail to reduce speed.
—Lay your weight backwards to take up a slightly crouching position on the back leg, at the same time tilting the sail backwards.
—Pull the board in front of your body with the front foot and at the same time kick the stern round behind you.
—Push your weight forward and move the rig in the same direction.
—Start with the clew forward.
—Shift the sail.
—Change your foot position.

Pivot gybe. Round up (1) and luff the sail briefly to lose speed and thus dynamic lift. Lean your weight back (2), and continue to lean well back while bearing off (3).

Pivot gybe continues as the stern is turned through the wind by a strong kick to leeward from the back foot (4). Change foot positions and with weight and clew forward sail off and gybe the sail (5–7).

6

7

EXPERT SAILING TECHNIQUES

E: extreme sailors

When you have a safe command of the basic and advanced techniques it is possible to specialize in the techniques of extreme windsurfing:

—Sailing in flat water with the slalom sinker. For this you must become familiar with sinker technique and trim. You can learn the 360° turn and the one-handed gybe.

—Speed surfing. The emphasis here is on optimum control of your 'gun', its trim and that of the sail and rig.

—Sailing in breakers. Here the emphasis is on getting used to breakers. Wave judgement has to be learned. You must know how to

sail out safely and, much more important, how to get safely back to the beach. To this add wave-riding manoeuvres: cut-back, bottom turn, traversing and jumping.

All these surfing specialities are sailed on sinkers or marginal boards. The emphasis in sinker sailing is not primarily on sailing technique. Above all, it requires great awareness of safety requirements and great ability to judge sea and wind conditions, as in an emergency you have much less chance of rescue than with a board of ample buoyancy. In saying this we don't want to frighten you off: these boards offer opportunities for so many different experiences that you should not let the chance pass to sail one. If you sail them sensibly, you

will not be in any danger. The windsurfer who is in great danger is the one who, full of enthusiasm for sinker sailing, the 'special' conditions and his own superb ability, rushes off blindly into the water without making a realistic evaluation of the conditions and his ability to cope with them. No true experts in any sport do this. That is why the good windsurfers seldom have accidents, unless they collide with someone or their equipment.

Sinker Technique

The greatest problem when sailing a sinker is to maintain the necessary dynamic lift, so that the board always has enough speed to plane. This is why a sinker can only be sailed in winds constantly over Force 4. In

sailing areas where the wind sometimes drops below this you should leave your sinker on the car roof. In any event you must know the flaws and wind shadows in your area. Pure sinkers can only rarely be used on inland waters, though they have proved their qualities above all in breaking waves.

In order to be able to use your skills to keep the board planing as well as possible, attach the boom to the mast no higher than eye-level. This will give you better control of the rig. A greater height is unnecessary anyway, since the shortness of the board makes you stand by the mast and the boom height is not so much reduced when raking the rig back as on a longer board.

The reduced buoyancy in all parts of the board, and its shorter length, mean that it can be tilted in any direction. The correct weighting of the board and the correct rig position are therefore decisive for speed. At full speed your weight should be equally distributed between the back foot and the boom, on which you hang. The rig is raked back and pulled slightly to windward. If your weight leans too far back the stern will begin to sink; too much weight on the boom will make the bow dig in. This can also happen if you let the rig hang too far forward.

The difference between a good planing position and sinking or digging in is very small, because the board is very sensitive to shifts of weight. You must therefore be very agile on your board, as any reduction in dynamic lift towards the stern, caused for example by reduced speed, must be compensated by stepping forward. Otherwise the stern will sink with you completely. On the other hand, at the onset of a gust you must at once move backwards from your position by the mast in order to prevent the bow diving under.

Sinkers are also much more sensitive to foot-steering movements. These are basically the same as are used on other boards without a daggerboard, but you must get used to the fact that a sinker will react to your weighting an edge with a sharp and radical change of direction. If you don't counter the centrifugal force which then hits you with an 'inside' position (see photos), and stay leaning to the inside of the turn, it will throw you from the board. Manoeuvres on sinkers involve tighter turns than on normal funboards.

Sailing a sinker requires a highly developed sense of safety, above all on the sea coast. Since the board will not support your weight when it is stationary or going slowly, you must always take precautions. Here are some of the essential rules of sinker sailing:
—You must achieve secure mastery of the beach start, water start and power gybe.
—Check your equipment for damage before setting out.
—Never sail in an offshore wind.
—Never sail with an offshore current.
—Know your sailing area thoroughly.
—Always have somebody watching you.
—Never go farther out than 200 m from the beach.
—Before setting out, first observe the conditions for a few minutes. If you have the slightest doubt, stay on shore.

As a sinker pilot you must definitely be a good, fit swimmer: sailors going into breakers should be able to swim for at least one hour. You must also be able to paddle your board in strong winds and high waves.

In an emergency, it is better when paddling back to lose the rig rather than your life.

The One-handed Gybe

The one-handed gybe is not really a separate manoeuvre. The sequence is the same as for the power gybe, the only difference being that the grip is slightly changed.

The mast hand holds the boom beside the mast. The sail hand hangs free or, when the clew swings forward, is held on the lee side ('hand washing'). Sometimes the windsurfer presses against the forward part of the boom with his elbow, in order to prevent the sail feathering early.

The one-handed gybe has no particular function in normal slalom surfing, except that it is highly photogenic, but it gains points in World Cup wave-riding competitions. For this you must lean well into the turn and stretch out.

To sail a one-handed gybe you need plenty of speed.

—Sail on your fastest reaching heading or in front of a wave. The mast hand grips the mast.
—Move your back foot to leeward and bear away by shifting your weight forward and at an angle, making a wide turn to leeward.
—The sail hand lets go of the boom.
—When the clew has swung forward past the 90° position stretch out, push the rig to shoulder height and dip the other hand into the water.
—Grip the other side of the boom with the new mast hand if the rig threatens to be pulled out of your hand.
—Let the rig hang for a moment to leeward and towards the stern, then pull it in the plane of the sail to windward, change your foot position and haul in with the sail hand.

It is important to maintain your speed throughout the manoeuvre so that the stern will not slide out of the turn.

One-handed sailing and 'hand washing' is also possible in a duck gybe. A two-grip technique is the best:

—Bear away to a reaching course by moving your weight at an angle forwards and to leeward.
—The mast hand grasps the other side of the boom, under the sail foot.
—The sail hand is released and hangs down in the water to leeward, while the other hand pulls the rig back a little.
—The free hand is quickly drawn out of the water and takes the boom.
—The sail is hauled in tight
—Foot positions change.

Variation
Sail a duck gybe using one of the three-grip techniques described above. The sail hand, which reaches first under the sail foot, grips the boom near the sail's pressure point and balances the rig. The other hand is dipped in the water.

One-handed gybe. The rig is held in balance by one hand on the middle of the boom while the free hand is 'washed' (left). Foot positions are changed after shifting over the sail.

360° Turn

The most important condition for this is maximum speed, which carries you through the whole manoeuvre. The turn can only be sailed with strong foot steering, as for more than half the time you must press the sail towards the water in order to avoid being pushed backwards by the rig.

For the highest possible speed you must, exactly as in a duck gybe, select the best place to make your 360°. The best conditions are:

360° turn, demonstrated by Jürgen in heavy conditions (from right). Bear away by leaning inward; the sail stays hauled in. It will be pushed down to the water once the board has passed through the downwind position. The mast is raked back, the sail's foot stays close to the board (1–3). Once back closehauled on the original tack, the sail is raised to a driving position (4–6).

6   5   4

—areas of flat water
—smooth water between two waves
—hanging on the front of a wave (with the wind at an angle off-shore).

The sequence:
—Set the back foot to leeward and weight the lee rail as you would for a carved gybe; the sail stays in tight all the time you are bearing away.
—Once the wind is astern, lay your body weight on the rig: the mast is pressed towards the water and the foot of the sail comes nearer the board (mast raked back).
—Shortly before the bow is pointing into the wind slowly lift the rig.
—When in the eye of the wind transfer your weight to the back foot and use it to kick the stern around behind your body, while the front foot pulls the board around in front (see sinker gybe).
—Haul the sail in tight and push it slightly over the bow, then proceed on your old course.

The decisive point is shortly before the sail turns over from a backed to a normal position. The rig is standing in an unsuitable position to resume pulling, and at this point there is also usually no momentum left to sail on.

While giving the board the final kick you must therefore try to bring the rig to a vertical position without any wind pressure on it.

If there is enough momentum for a 270° turn and the wind is not so

3   2   1

strong, you can carry out the rest of the turn with the sail slightly more upright, backed and leaning towards the stern.

Speed Sailing

One extreme development is speed trials. You will doubtless be familiar with such competitions, held on the sea or on inland waters. The speed on courses from wind abeam to close-hauled is usually decisive, and the boards are designed accordingly. Very few go onto a broad-reaching course, probably because of fear of having to beat back up or perhaps of the spectacular falls which can then happen. However, these are the courses where you can experience the amazing speeds of which a windsurfer is capable. The boards most suitable for this, which can cut choppy waves as well as sail in smooth water, are 'guns' between 2.30 and 3.0 m long, less than 55 cm wide, with straight edge lines aft of the mast, and are designed for pure speed. They can only be gybed in a wide curve, and their manoeuvrability would be unsatisfactory for slalom. On the other hand they sail fast and relatively smoothly. The Vee, slight rocker and sometimes concave bottom towards the stern allow you to haul in the sail tighter without the board breaking out sideways when you press laterally against it.

Riding guns is one of the great thrills of windsurfing on funboards. Guns don't allow very sharp mano-euvres, but it is still a great feeling to have full speed after a carved gybe. Broad-reaching on a gun shows you the high-speed poten-tial of boards.

BASIC SURFING AND JUMPING

Selecting a Site

For your initial forays into surf it's very important to choose a suitable site. Hookipa at 10 ft is not the place to start. Instead, a place with a moderate sideshore wind (blowing parallel to the shoreline), a sandy beach and small mushy waves that break some distance from shore is ideal for learning.

It's important that the waves are not breaking very close to the beach, for two reasons: you'll have difficulty launching, and when you surf a wave in you'll have no opportunity to turn around – the white water will sweep you onto the shore. Ideally waves should break 50 to 100 m offshore, then reach slightly deeper water between the shore and the break. In the deeper water the white water will dissipate, leaving room to tack or gybe without having to worry about a surge of white water knocking you down.

Stick with mushy, rolling waves at first. They're less powerful than hollow waves of the same size, and they break more slowly and predictably. Where a hollow wave might snap your mast, a mushy one won't.

If the wind is too much onshore you'll have difficulty getting out past the white water. If it's too much offshore you'll be unable to catch a wave. The more nearly the wind is parallel with the faces of the waves, the more easily you'll be able to punch through the white water and the more easily you'll be able to catch and surf a wave in.

If the wind is side-onshore (onshore at an angle to the beach) and the waves are not swell but rather breaking seas, you'll probably find that most of them break in a rolling

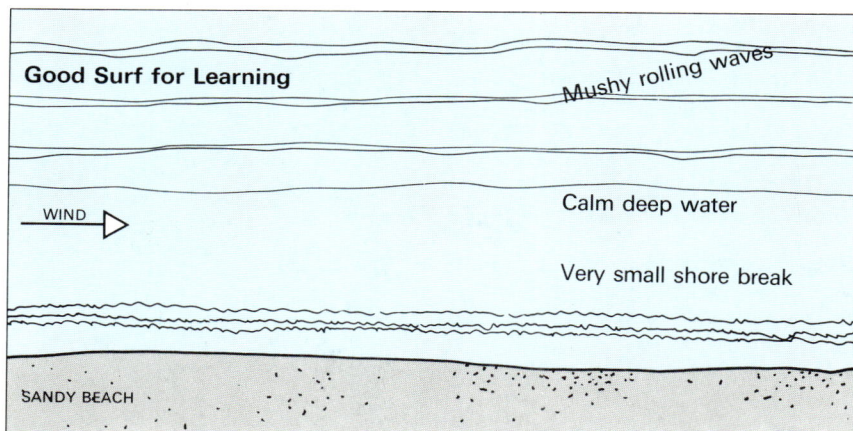

fashion, while a few are very hollow. Look out for the hollow ones. They occur when one wave catches up with a slower-moving smaller one and the two suddenly create one big wave. The effect is the same as if the bottom had suddenly become much shallower: the wave hollows and breaks powerfully.

Things to avoid are: jetties, piers, people fishing, high waves, winds that are directly offshore, and a big shore break. Also steer clear of wave-riders and surfboarders.

Launching

The best way if your board is fairly big and the shore break is small is shown here. Other methods are described later.

When launching off a beach into surf there are several important points. The pause or 'smooth' between two wave sets has to be used, and running and jumping onto the board helps give you enough speed before meeting the first oncoming set.

Good Surf for Learning — Mushy rolling waves — Calm deep water — Very small shore break — WIND — SANDY BEACH

Going Out

In small waves with a sideshore wind, going out is fairly easy. When you encounter your first surge of white water, however, you'll probably feel like you've run aground and go tumbling over the bow. The correct way to handle the surge is: first, make sure your board is perpendicular to it; second, rock your weight back onto your back foot just before hitting the surge; and third, luff your sail briefly just before you hit it then sheet in as you go over.

If the wind is side-offshore the same advice applies. The only differences are that you'll have to bear away a bit in order to meet the white water squarely, and your weight shift and luffing must be more pronounced.

If the wind is side-onshore your technique must be different. As you approach a surge you must head up sharply so that your board is more nearly perpendicular to the surge. Then, as you cross the white water you must bear away quickly to regain speed. It is important to bear away enough so that you are at full speed when you hit the next surge: without good speed you won't make it over.

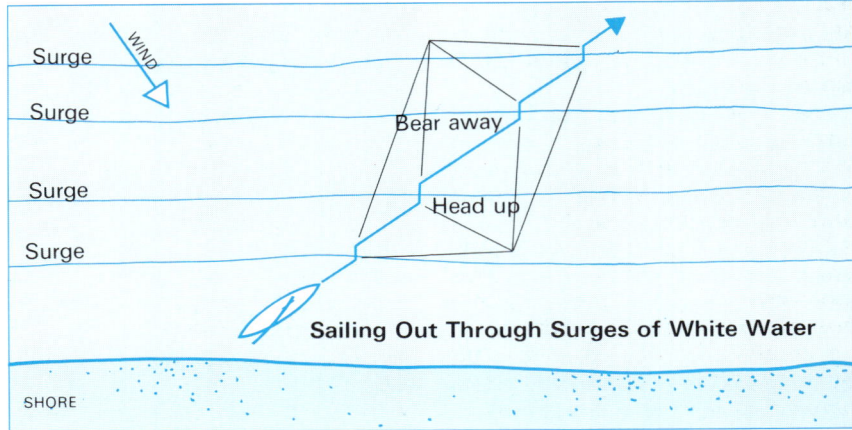

Also, when you hit the surge you should lift the windward rail of your board so that it will glide up over it. Otherwise the white water may catch the rail and carry you shoreward.

If you're caught sideways-on to the white water, or have no speed, you're sure to fall. So keep up your speed by bearing away, then meet the surge head-on by heading up.

When you're nearly outside the break you'll encounter waves that are about to break or are breaking. A wave is most powerful at the point where it is breaking, so at first you should steer away from that point — the critical section. Reach the wave where it has already broken or is yet to grow and break.

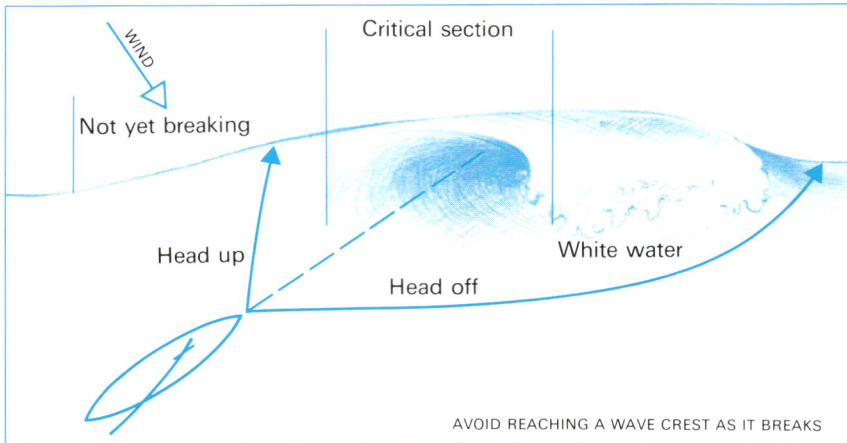

Sailing Out Through Surges of White Water

SHORE

AVOID REACHING A WAVE CREST AS IT BREAKS

2

Jumping

As long as you have lots of wind, jumping is fairly easy. It's landing that can be difficult.

The first time you go wave-jumping you don't want to get twenty feet up in the air. Anything could go wrong and you'd crash. Find a place with a sideshore wind, sail with good speed toward a peak which is about to break, then just as you go up the face of the wave shift most of your weight to your back leg, luff your sail and tilt it forward slightly. Luffing keeps you from jumping too high and tilting it forward prevents heading up. You'll become briefly airborne as you leave the wave crest, then drop immediately back to the water. As soon as you're back on the water sheet in and continue. The advantages of taking this approach are: you can avoid a lot of falls and thus learn more quickly (recovering from falls is time-consuming); you acquire the feel for luffing and sheeting your sail before and after a jump; you'll get the feel for landing tail-first, especially important when you're learning because it produces the least stress on your board, legs and back.

One good place to use this jumping technique is in slalom competition when the wind is side-shore and very strong. To get from an inside buoy to an outside one as quickly as possible, it doesn't pay to hit the steep waves at full speed and get big jumps. Luffing over the steep ones is less spectacular but much faster.

Once you're comfortable with luffing through jumps, you're ready to try some higher ones. The approach to the wave should be fast; try to steer so that you meet the steepest portion of the wave. Again, shift your weight to your back foot, but this time push off with that foot just as you reach the crest of the wave. At the same time luff briefly, then sheet in again. Sailing fast into the steepest part of the wave and then pushing off with your back foot will assure a high jump, and being sheeted in as much as possible will keep you in the air longer. However, luffing just as you leave the water will help to keep from heading up and/or nose-diving. Tilting up the windward rail also helps control heading-up tendencies and can even cause you to head off. Heading off a bit in the air, as explained earlier, can prevent spinout on landing.

One jumping technique that works well with large boards (over 10 ft long) is to lock your body into its takeoff position for the duration of the jump.

Jumping through the shore break

Here are a few more points to keep in mind:

-Don't land with one rail significantly lower than the other. You could trip over it and have a bad fall.
-Flat landings maintain speed but can break boards. To achieve a flat landing you should pull your feet up just before touchdown.
-If you find yourself out of control you should bail out and push the board away from you. The wind will probably blow the board away, but still look out for it.
-Since your feet are locked into footstraps you can easily hurt an ankle or foot. Use great caution.
-When you bail out you should avoid landing flat on your back, stomach or side. Landing incorrectly could knock the wind out of you. So always break the water with an arm or leg as you enter it, or curve your body (as in judo falls).
-Don't have your harness hooked in while jumping.

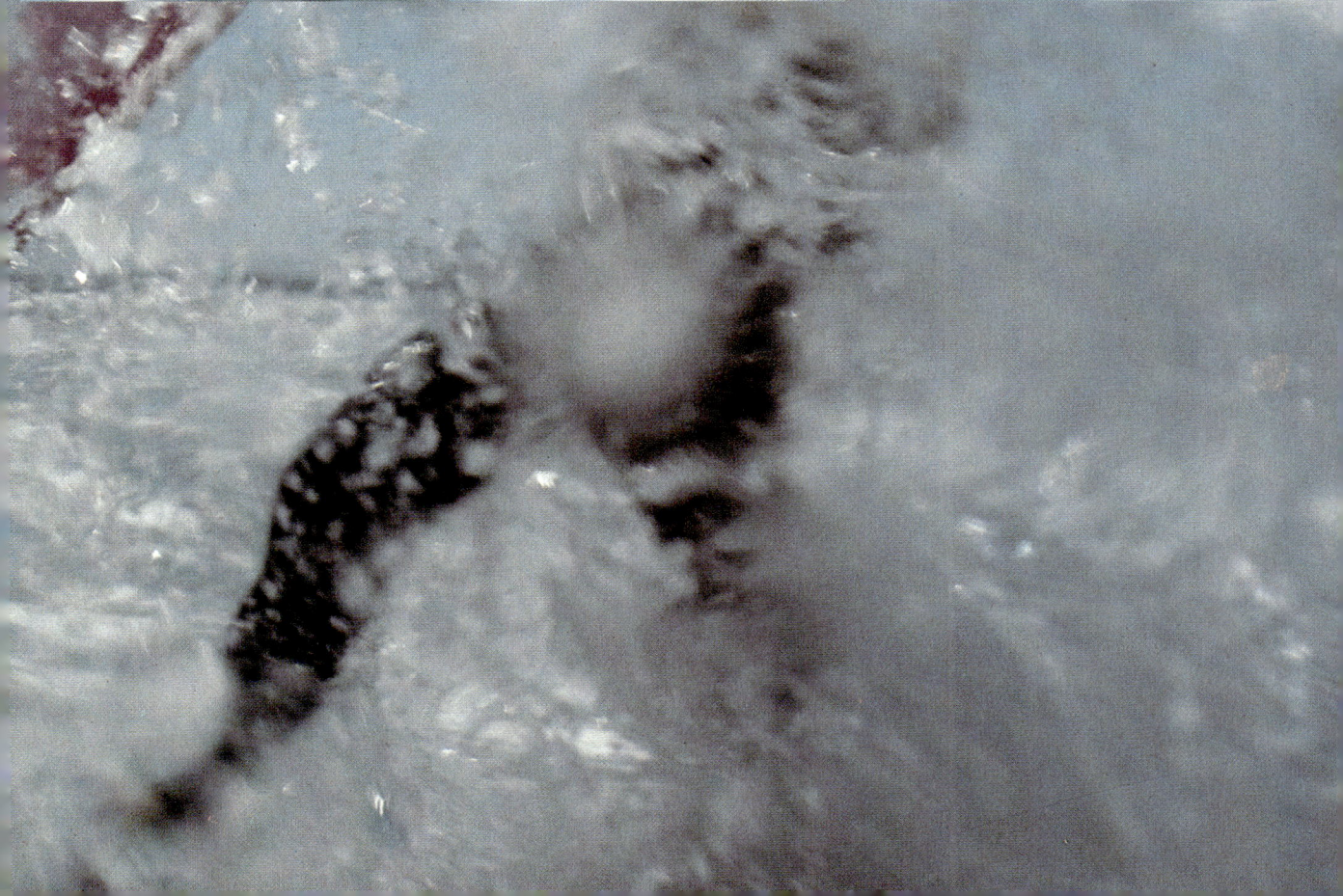

Coming in to the Shore

Getting back to the beach is much easier to do without mishap than going out. You simply carve a snappy gybe and sail in. What can get you into trouble, though, is inadvertently coming too close to the critical section of a wave, or not realizing that a wave is about to break as you sail down the face.

First, you must always watch the waves very closely so that you can acquire a feel for when they will break, where they will break first, and how powerfully. Getting 'wave judgement' is the most important thing you can do in the waves. It will help you get through big surf and it'll help you get good jumps and make your surfing look good no matter what level you're at technically.

Second, as you sail toward the beach position yourself low down on the face of a wave. Keep the stern of the board right about where the wave starts to slope up steeply. This is a safe position and a good one from which to observe the wave become steeper and finally break. When the wave approaches what you consider to be 'critical' steepness and it's just about to break, you should accelerate a bit to stay ahead of the wave and away from the portion that is actually breaking.

Third, slow down a little after the wave has broken and let the white water push you along. Head up, bear away, luff your sail, get a feel for how the white water acts on your board. Continue in until the surge subsides (assuming you've had the good fortune to find a site where the white water subsides before reaching the beach), carve another snappy gybe and prepare to head back out.

If you do succeed in finding a place with this zone of deep water, you'll notice that the water is very smooth in the area where the white water is constantly sweeping past, but very choppy where the white water stops. As you become more confident in your gybes you'll want to do them on the smooth area between the surges of white water, rather than in the safe but bumpy water inside.

Wave-riding

Just sailing toward the beach in front of a wave is not surfing it. To surf in the proper sense means performing turns on the face, drop from top to bottom, climb back up to the top, bank off the white water and do all these as high on the face and as near the critical section of the wave as possible.

This may sound a little arbitrary to the novice, but in fact describes those aspects of surfing that offer the greatest thrill and fun. In performing such manoeuvres you experience the weightless sensation of falling as you drop down the face, followed by the G force of a tight, fast bottom turn.

By positioning yourself high on the wave you gain potential energy, which becomes kinetic energy as you drop down the face. Thus you tap three different and powerful sources of energy simultaneously. The *wind's* kinetic energy is captured with the proper use of sail and board. The motion of the *wave* gives you greater effective approach speed when you're jumping; also, the potential energy converted to kinetic energy as the wave breaks can be used by the good surfer and jumper. *Gravity* helps give you speed.

The most fun surfing is the highest power surfing, just as fast powerful cars are fun to drive. All those manoeuvres are not just some arcane ritual performed only by drug-crazed surf bums.

Wave-riding Terminology

Going right/left
'Going right' on a wave means: as you look from the sea to the beach, surfing to your right. Going the other way is 'going left'.

Backside/Frontside
When the wave is to your back, you are surfing 'backside'. When the sail is between you and the wave (in your normal sailing position), you're surfing 'frontside'. Where the wind comes from your left as you go out, you surf frontside when you're going left, backside when you're going right. Backside surfing is always done when the wind is onshore or side onshore; frontside is always done when the wind is side offshore. Both can be done when the wind is sideshore or within 20° of sideshore.

Surfing backside is quite natural and easy; it's the first type you should attempt. Instead of going straight towards the beach when you surf your next wave, do a bottom turn and traverse the wave face.

Bottom Turn

To do a bottom turn simply shift your weight aft slightly and tilt your windward rail down. To bottom turn sharply, move the heel of your back foot very near the windward rail, then shift most of your weight to that foot. The farther back and to windward you put your foot and the more weight you shift onto it, the sharper the turn will be.

Above: Jürgen is riding low on the wave, in a safe position in the trough. Left: he is near the critical section, sailing high.

93

Above: surfing frontside (left) and backside. Below: Ken in a bottom turn. He is sailing frontside and so has to bear off to get onto the wave again.

Opposite page: a gybe on the wall. You have to hold your extreme inside stance. The object is to do it up to the lip of the wave.

Traversing

Once you've completed a gentle bottom turn you'll find yourself traversing the face of the wave much the way a skier traverses a hill. Weighting the windward side will make the rail edge into the water, and the bow will be pointing down and along the face of the wave. Traversing is not the most interesting thing you can be doing: once you're experienced, you'll traverse only when you have to work upwind or get past white water.

Cutback (backside)

To turn back down the wave you perform a cutback. An easy, gentle turn requires no more than tilting the leeward rail down by pressing with your toes. For a sharper, more dramatic cutback, as when you are heading up the wave face and want to drop back down again, you have to shift your weight and angle your board the way you would to initiate a gybe. As you come out of your bottom turn your weight will be to windward, but to do a cutback you need your weight to be over and slightly to leeward of the board.

Weight the windward rail momentarily so the board steers up under you; at the same time sheet in a bit more for a second so that the sail pulls you to leeward. These two actions will position your body so that all you have to do is push down on the toes of your back foot and you'll cut back down the wave.

To cutback quickly and sharply, get your weight way back (a quick luff of the sail helps) and put a lot of pressure on your back foot. Keeping your weight forward will cause you to turn more slowly, but also more smoothly.

Landing
There are numerous ways to come in and land on the beach. The photos show an easy, safe method that works well in all conditions and with all sizes of boards. (See page 97.)

1

Page 96, right to left: Ken demonstrates a roller-coaster. He does a bottom turn towards the wave and into its critical section (1, 2). He then makes his turn back where the wave is capping (breaking), but gets pushed farther into the turn by the white water and is carried away.

Page 97: to make a landing, step off your board in knee-deep water and push it in towards shore. Lift the stern by the footstrap and turn it 180° round the bow, staying upwind of the sail. Walk it backwards out of the water.

COMPETITION
E: experts

In funboard sailing racing on the traditional Olympic-type triangular course or freestyle competition does not exist. Generally regattas are organized on the lines of the Euro-Funboard Cup or World Cup, the rules of which are very similar. These test to a far greater degree the qualities which distinguish funboards. The competitions include course racing, slalom and wave-riding. In the course races 20 per cent at the most consists of beating upwind (as against 50 per cent in Olympic triangle courses). The number of tacks is usually reduced to two, the number of gybes is about 16 to 18. The slalom is raced as a standard figure-of-eight slalom in the breaker area near the beach or, also in the breakers, in zig-zag lines from windward to leeward. Mastery of the board is not demonstrated by acrobatics, as in freestyle, but rather by playing with the board in the breakers while wave-riding.

Course Racing

Races are held on a course with long reaching legs and short upwind legs. The part before the wind is divided in a gybe slalom. Races are only started in 15 knots of wind or more. A competition consists of three to six races. The winner of each one receives 0.75 points and the points for the others are the same as their positions. When the points have been added up the sailor with the lowest total is the winner of this part of the competition. For an overall win the other parts are also decisive.

Slalom Racing

The slalom is only started in winds of at least 20 knots. The start is in groups of four to eight competitors and results are decided according to a knock-out system. The best sailors in each group qualify for the next round, until the best meet in the final. Sometimes a double knock-out system is offered, where the losers still have a chance to qualify in repechage

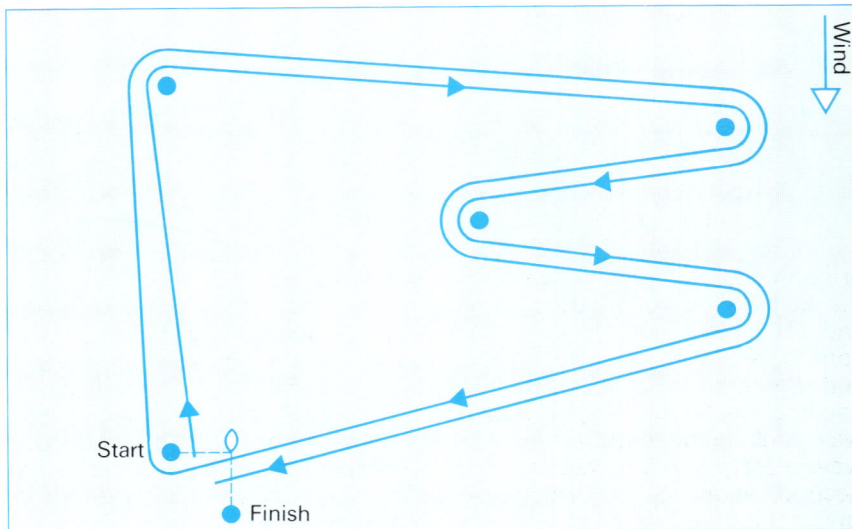

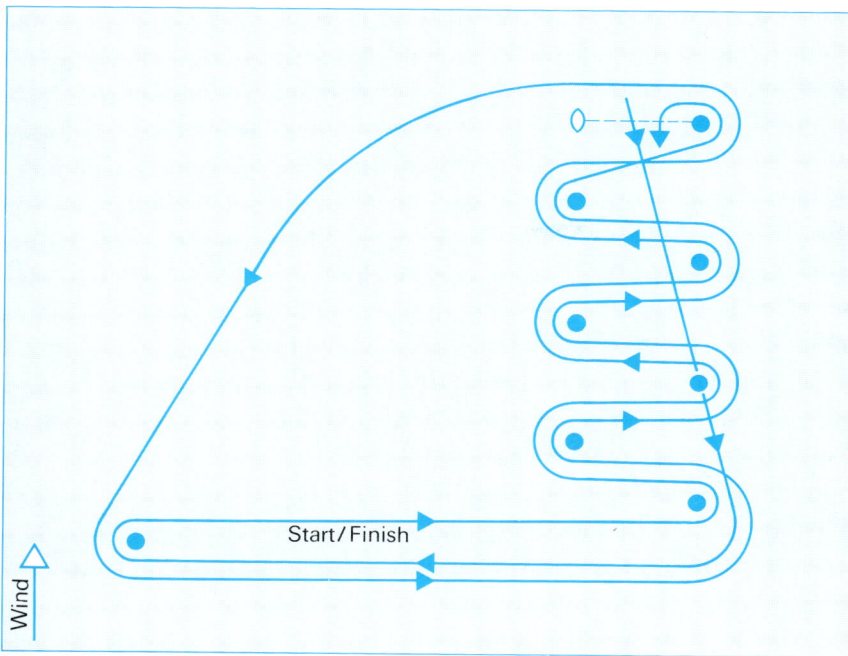

Start/Finish

Wind

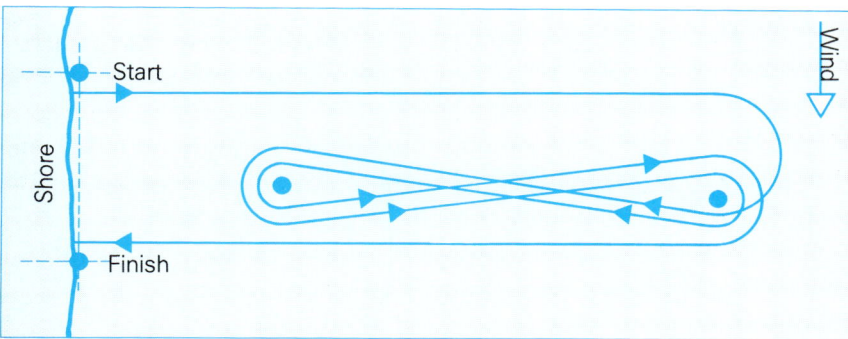

Start

Shore

Finish

Wind

these three categories ten points can be gained. Transitions are manoeuvres such as gybes, cutbacks and bottom turns, for which a maximum of thirty points can be achieved. Points are awarded by a jury. Here there is also a winner of each discipline, and according to the order points are distributed to find the overall winner.

The Points System
The three parts are not weighted equally for the overall scoring. Course racing and slalom contribute 40 per cent each, wave-riding 20 per cent to an overall win.

On the lines of the degree of difficulty of regattas, placings in the individual disciplines are awarded points according to Table A (for difficult races: course racing with more than three races and slalom and wave-riding with a double knock-out), or Table B (easier races with less than three runs or slalom and wave-riding with a straight knock-out), and these points are added up to give an annual ranking. This is how the Funboard European and World Champions are decided.

Euro-Funboard and World Cups
There is no basic difference between these two apart from the fact that while the competitor in the Euro-Funboard Cup has a free choice of equipment and takes part in important regattas in European sailing areas to qualify for the European Championship, the 'professionals' of the World Cup must use a common pool of equipment and decide the World Championship among themselves in seven regattas held all over the world. The Euro-Funboard Cup is officially an amateur competition, the World Cup for professionals.

or consolation races. The winner in the slalom discipline is thus found, and the points which he receives contribute to the overall score. Here and in wave-riding you must know two important rules. First, the right of way is different: whoever is on a wave must give way to those in front. Second, at marks the two board-length rule does not apply.

Wave-riding
Wave-riding competition can be started in wind speeds from 12 knots upwards. It is not decided by such objective criteria as finishing order. The windsurfers have about ten minutes each in which to demonstrate their ability in the breakers. Points are given for wave-riding, jumps and transitions: for each of

Speed Trials

Every year speed competitions take place in Weymouth (UK), Brest (F) and Knokke (NL) in which attempts are made to beat the maximum sailing speed records. The record has been held for some years by the English proa *Crossbow II* (37 knots), and in 1983 the record for windsurfers was 30.82 knots.

The rules for a speed trial are simple. A circuit of markers is laid out, with corridors 500 m long. In Weymouth the timed area can be watched from the shore. The sailor must attempt to cover the measured distance as quickly as possible. There is no limit to the number of attempts or the equipment used. If a speed is 2 per cent faster than the old record it is registered as a new one. The percentage difference is to allow for the possibility of inexact timing or course variations due to moving markers.

Jürgen at Weymouth in 1982, after which he held the world speed record for a short time.

Equipment

Boards with extremely low volume and weight (4–5 kg) have proved successful in speed trials. The rig should be a winger sail on a stiff, tapered and faired mast. The booms are wide apart so that one can use body weight without leaning the rig to windward. The sail must be as large as possible.

The technique

In speed sailing the rig is pulled slightly to windward. It leans towards the stern and is sheeted in as tightly as possible. Your body weight is transferred as far as possible from the feet to the rig, so that the board is on the verge of taking off and also of spinning out. You must avoid jumps. Spinout tendencies are compensated for by using light foot pressure on the lee edge.

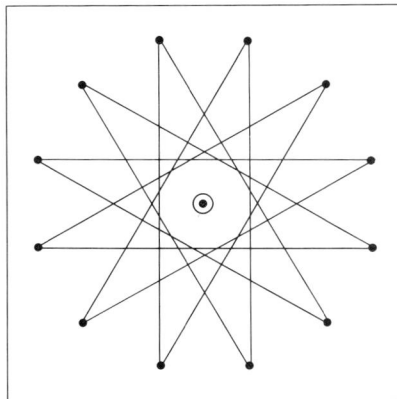

The timed and measured speed courses at Weymouth, laid out in Portland Harbour. The 'clock face' course has twelve possible lanes.

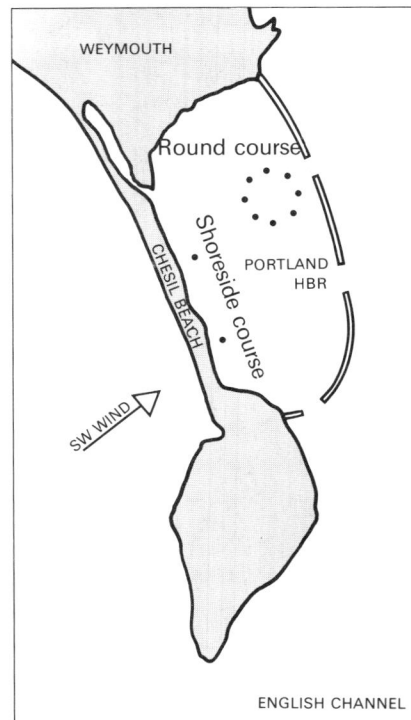

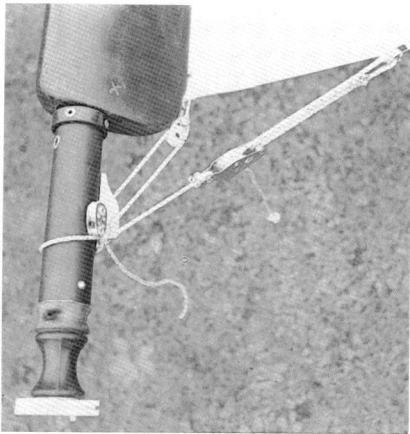

Tactics

Under 20 knots wind speed a world record is just about impossible. You should therefore not only aim for this. Keep the regatta win in mind and be sure to have one or two fast runs in what you consider to be the best conditions of the day, otherwise you will end up in the same situation as many top sailors at Knokke: on the first day the wind was under Force 6 so they hardly sailed at all but rather waited for stronger winds. On the following days the wind died down even more, so that the fastest person from the first day went home with victory and the prize money.

You should also avoid the other extreme, however. Many runs will give you a lot of times, but will cost you a lot of strength. Your board is over-rigged, so in extreme conditions you will be able to stand no more than five runs of a consistently high quality.

The course is only 500 m long parallel to the marker lines, so try if possible to avoid sailing on a diagonal within the corridor. On entering the measured distance you must already be going maximum speed. It is worthwhile to sail into a gust which spreads over the whole course. You can only produce your maximum effort when you are thoroughly warm, so make sure that you have appropriate protection against the cold, keep warm between runs (hot tea, etc) and move about. If you start to feel cold or perhaps even shiver, you may just as well stop.

Ken's wing rig, showing the airfoil section mast, the connection between mast and boom, and the adjusting lines.

The standard World Cup course has an adequate windward leg, a moderate number of gybes, four different points of sailing on the reaches, and it is relatively easy to set.

EQUIPMENT

Boards

The board must be large enough to plane readily in Force 4, yet small enough to be controllable in Force 8. It must have the upwind speed of an Open Class Division II board, and the reaching speed of a speed board. It must be as light as possible, yet stiff and strong enough to withstand jumping and pounding.

A successful race board is typically about 65 cm wide and 3.60–4.00 m long. Length allows good windward ability in a wide range of wind strengths and gives directional stability. Width is a compromise between the quick planing ability of a very wide hull and the high-speed control of a narrow one.

The bottom The back half has a slightly Veed bottom which blends into a moderate amount of round in the bow. The Vee tends to make the board more easily driven upwind, improves tracking and resistance to spinout on the reaches, and reduces the board's tendency to pitch up and

1

2

103

down on a high-speed reach in rough water. The roundness forward improves windward ability, especially in lighter winds, and if correctly distributed can improve offwind performance. However, if the bow is too round or too flat, or if the roundness is incorrectly distributed across the width of the board, it will be slowed excessively every time the bow touches the water. The chines on the forward half of the bottom are intended to deflect spray away from the hull.

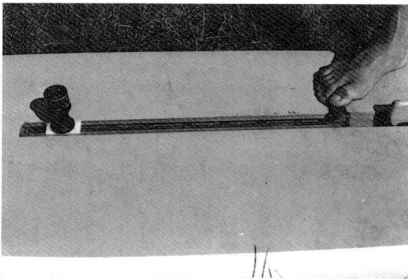

The ends at both bow and stern are fairly narrow, around 32–37 cm wide at a point 30 cm from each end, and the outline is curved gently in the back to improve gybing. Narrowness forward reduces weight, windage and wetted surface; a narrow stern reduces wetted surface, improves directional stability at high speed and lessens the tendency to spinout.

The rocker For the back 1.50–1.80 m of the board the rocker is flat, then rises gradually to about 30 cm of scoop in the bow. The distribution of rocker has a profound effect on board performance. A board with a long straight span will plane quickly and will be fastest on flat water and close-reaching. With less straight rocker in the back it will be superior in stronger winds, rougher water and on broader, faster reaches.

The centreboard The fully retracting type is a feature of all race boards. Wetted surface is reduced for reaching and the tendency to head up uncontrollably or spinout is greatly reduced. Sometimes a board will be equipped with two or more centreboards, the larger of which retracts only 80 per cent of the way. Since the larger centreboard is used only in light winds when reaching speeds aren't very great, it's not bad to have the extra lateral resistance afforded by a partially retracted centreboard. In winds of more than Force 4, however, the fully retractable type is best.

Mast tracks are also found on all race boards. Since lowering the centreboard moves the centre of lateral resistance forward for upwind sailing, the centre of effort, the sail, must be moved forward as well. If the mast has only one location the sailor must tilt the sail forward at an awkward and inefficient angle in order to avoid heading up too much while beating. The mast track allows the CE to be moved forward while leaving the mast at a comfortable and efficient angle for the sailor. The other advantages of moving the mast foot forward for windward sailing are:
—The mast is tilted in such a way that one can hang more of his weight on the boom and thus carry a bigger sail.
—The downward force of the mast in its forward position holds the bow of the board down, thus keeping the stern from sinking and causing excessive drag.
—Railing tendency is reduced, allowing larger sails and centreboards to be used.

Raising the centreboard and planing with the front half of the board out of the water moves the CLR aft, so the sail too must be moved aft. Just tilting the sail back isn't good enough because the clew is likely to drag in the water, and the pressure of the mast in its forward position tends to drive the bow down and increase wetted surface. The mast track allows moving the foot of the mast aft, leaving the board and sail in good trim.

Skegs are frequently neglected and misunderstood, but one of the most important parts of the board. Upwind, you need a large effective skeg in order to hold a straight, fast course through gusts and waves. On a reach you need a large effective one to prevent even the slightest degree of spinout.

Footstraps, between six and ten, are mounted on every race board; usually two or four for sailing upwind and four to six for reaching. Their exact arrangement depends on the sailor's personal style and the board design. It's best to have only the straps you absolutely need and no more. Otherwise the board becomes a nightmare to sail in marginal planing conditions when you don't need to be in the straps but do need some uncluttered space on which to stand.

The Rig
A really good rig means a fast sail. But in order to have a fast sail you need a light, strong, stiff mast. It should be very light so you can raise the sail without pulling a muscle, and it must be strong so as not to be easily broken when you fall at high speed or get caught by a breaking sea. Most important, however, it must be stiff so that the sail doesn't twist excessively

and so it keeps its shape.

Carbon fibre masts provide the best stiffness to weight ratio and are, if properly constructed, amply strong. Some aluminium masts are reasonably stiff, but can not be made as stiff as the carbon ones without being too heavy.

Sails for racing, a set would include the following:

no.	sq m		sq ft approx.
1—	7.1	sq m *or*	78 sq ft approx.
2—	6.4		70
3—	5.7		62
4—	4.9		54
5—	4.2		46
6—	3.5		38

Heavy air racing sails should generally be quite stable in shape, strongly built of Mylar or firmly woven sailcloth so that they don't stretch and change shape in a gust. Full-length battens also help to stabilize shape. This is important because wind energy expended in stretching cloth or bending a mast is not used for driving the board over the water, and it distorts the sail from its optimum shape.

The booms should be very stiff, fit the mast snugly and with little wobble and should allow adjustment of the outhaul while sailing. The stiffness allows the sail to keep its shape in a gust, and the snug fit to the mast facilitates good tacking and gybing. The adjustable outhaul accommodates wind strength changes and different points of sailing. Sheaves in the clew end fitting lower friction and give a good mechanical advantage for tensioning the outhaul.

The universal joint should swivel freely at both ends and should be of a type that doesn't break. The mast foot should allow a lot of down-haul tension and easy adjustment.

Wing masts were a new development in 1983; a carbon fibre reinforced spar with the cross-section of an airfoil. Such masts greatly improve rig efficiency and increase potential speed. Within a month of the wing mast's introduction it was instrumental in the setting of a new world speed record for sailboards.

Above: the mast is moved forward for close-reaching. Below: the position for a broad reach.

Tuning

In properly setting up your windsurfer for a particular leg of the course you must be concerned with the selection of sail and daggerboard, and the correct adjustment of these and the mast foot position.

Sail Selection

Obviously sail choice depends on the wind strength on the course but also on anticipated changes in wind and sea conditions. During the 1983 San Francisco World Cup I started the first race of the second day with a 70 sq ft (6.4 sq m) sail. The wind increased so much that by the second beat I was barely able to sail at all. Phillip Pudenz, on the other hand, anticipating the wind increase had wisely rigged a smaller sail than mine and was romping to an easy win. Ironically, the race ultimately had to be abandoned due to lack of wind.

The mistake I and many other sailors made was to underestimate the vigor with which the sea breeze would fill in that afternoon. We should have known, given the starting time of the race, the weather forecast and the pre-race conditions, that the wind would soon be too much for 70 sq ft sails.

Sea conditions also affect sail choice. Where the water is basically flat, i.e. there are no large, steep, open ocean swells, a sail that is somewhat large and overpowering for a given wind strength can be effectively used. In Kailua Bay, Hawaii or La Torche, France, however, where the seas can be quite large, it's best to avoid being overpowered.

The type of course to be sailed can also affect sail selection. The O'Neill Classic consists mostly of beam and broad reaching, frequently in winds that diminish toward the end of the course. Thus it's best to take the biggest sail possible: if you can get through the first two triangles you're sure to move up fast on the reaches. In contrast, the Euro-Funboard course requires a lot of close-reaching and gybing so it's best to not be overpowered. As a general rule, aim to be slightly overpowered in the gusts so that you have to feather or luff the sail somewhat.

Sail Trim

Most windsurfer sails have few shape controls, so simply flattening it with the outhaul and eliminating horizontal wrinkles on the luff by tensioning the downhaul is all you can usually do. The exact flatness needed depends on the wind strength, the water, the particular sail, the type of course and your style of sailing. The best way to determine the fastest settings is by sailing with a friend who is willing to act as a trial horse.

The rules that govern sail adjustment for boards are complex and imperfectly understood. They are similar in some ways to the rules that apply to dinghy sails, but not entirely. For example, tightening the outhaul of a sailboard sail necessarily tightens the leech; the same is not true of dinghy sails.

In general, however, in wind at the lower end of your sail's range, or if the water is unusually rough, your sail should be fairly full. Even sailing upwind, too flat a sail will hurt both speed and pointing. As the wind increases your sail should be flattened, until it's time to switch to a smaller one.

Beating and close-reaching require the flattest sails, while beam and broad-reaching require perhaps a 10 per cent increase in depth of camber.

The importance of these adjustments is greatest when you are using a big sail, something in the 60–80 sq ft (5.6–7.1 sq m) range. If conditions require you to use a 40 or 50 sq ft sail factors other than its precise adjustment will be more likely to determine your speed.

Don't underestimate the importance of correct sail adjustment in a race. In the 1983 Hang Ten Subaru regatta at Cabrillo Beach the wind was its strongest of the day at the start of the last race. So I flattened my sail slightly. My speed was fine the first time round, but by the second beat the wind had lightened a bit and both Alex Aguera and Robby Naish were catching up. We all reached the weather mark within a few lengths of each other, and as Robby sped away from me on the first reach (Alex had an equipment failure which may have cost him the regatta) I realized my sail was too flat. I slacked off the outhaul a bit and the change in my speed was as dramatic as it was quick. I immediately broke onto the plane, surfed a swell past Robby and held a widening lead to the finish. A slight change in fullness was all it took.

Centreboards

Your centreboard is most efficient when it is exactly the right size. The prototypes that I design and race come equipped with two. What I do is match the amount of blade under water to the size of my sail. For example, my large blade, 26 in deep by an average of about 6 in wide, goes with my 70 sq ft sail. The same blade pulled up 4 in in the centreboard well for upwind sailing works with my 62 sq ft sail. To go with my 54 and smaller sails I have a smaller blade – 20 in deep by an average of 5 in wide. These relationships will probably change in time, but for now they work quite well.

The blade should generally be vertical for sailing upwind and completely retracted on reaches. Although it's not currently fashionable to have a blade that only retracts 80 or 90 per cent of the way, there's really nothing wrong with such an arrangement as long as the wind is less than 20 knots. In fact for some of the close reaches commonly found on Euro-Funboard courses it is necessary to sail with the blade in a half down position. It's not a fast or fun way to sail, but the course requires it.

One thing to avoid whenever possible is sailing upwind with the blade swept aft more than a few inches. Sweepback reduces the tendency of the board to rail up or head up, chiefly by reducing the lift generated by the blade. It does not similarly reduce drag, however, so sweeping it aft is not as efficient as pulling it up vertically in the well.

Mast Track Adjustment

The mast foot should be in the forward most position (typically 8–8½ ft from the stern) for sailing upwind, and in the aftmost position (typically 6–6½ ft from the stern) for beam and broad reaching. Close-reaching with the centreboard up is generally done with the mast foot all the way back, while close-reaching with the blade half down is done with the mast foot halfway forward. If you are caught on the water with too large a sail and are having trouble staying on your feet, try reaching with the mast foot half or all the way forward. You won't be especially fast or comfortable, but you should make it back.

TECHNIQUE

Sailing upwind

Stance
Most of your weight should be on your back foot, while your front foot is generally somewhere on the rail according to personal style and the conditions. In light winds or flat water that front foot should be fairly close to the back one. Such a stance helps you to sail in precise balance. In strong or gusty winds or rough seas the front foot should be farther forward so that you can avoid being thrown by an exceptional wave or gust.

Since most weight is on the back foot it makes sense to always have that foot in a strap (except in very mild conditions). Strapped in, you can control railing more easily and won't be swept off by a passing wave. The front foot doesn't really have to be in a strap, though in very rough conditions it probably should be. On my race boards I have a special pointing strap for mild and moderate conditions that my back foot goes in. As the wind increases and I use smaller amounts of centre-board I move farther back on the board. The strap that had been for my back foot is then in a good place for my front foot, and my back foot goes into one of the reaching straps.

The front arm is usually straight, the back one slightly bent, with hands typically about shoulder width apart. The trapeze lines should be adjusted so that this arrangement of the arms is possible, and also so that your back arm takes a moderate load during gusts. Keeping your body at arms' length from the sail gives you a greater righting moment and thus allows you to harness more driving power from the wind.

Some sailors bend a great deal at the waist, others bend very little. Both have been successful. I prefer to bend a moderate amount.

It is important not to lean too much to windward and pull the sail over you like a wing. Doing so damages pointing ability. You don't want to go up into the air, you want to go upwind, so keep the rig as vertical as possible: it will be most efficient that way. The board, on the other hand, should be heeled slightly to leeward, but not nearly as much so as a Division II board – just a few degrees.

Holding a course
When you first start sailing a race board you should try to sail in a straight line on each tack. Gusts, lulls and waves will make control difficult; you'll probably be heading up and bearing away in a random, ineffective, slow way. So at first just try to go in a straight line without allowing the waves and gusts to alter your course. Practice first with a sail that you can easily control. Get the feel of the board and rig and how they respond to passing seas. When you can keep a steady course move up to a larger sail; learn to handle the gusts and lulls without loosing balance or changing course significantly. An important part of handling gusts is learning to 'feather'.

Feathering
Your sail should be large enough that during the gusts you have to luff slightly. This action I call 'feathering', even though it isn't quite the same as feathering the sail of a boat. The idea is to weather a gust without being rounded up and backwinded, without having to hike out excessively to windward, and without being catapulted. You have to observe the gust coming by keeping your eye on the patch of water just ahead and to

windward. When it hits, allow the sail to luff slightly and at the same time, in order to forstall the board's tendency to round up, tilt the sail forward slightly. Ride out the gust and watch for the ensuing lull.

Once you've spent some time on the board and are in good control start thinking about how to use the constant variations in wind and sea to best advantage.

Gusts

Windsurfers are very light and responsive and can accelerate quickly in a gust, so your reactions must be quick and correct. If you are already planing when a gust hits (assuming there is no change in wind direction) you should: (1) luff, if necessary, to accommodate the greater wind strength; (2) maintain your heading or bear away just a bit to accelerate and allow for the slight heading by the wind that accompanies the increase in true wind; and (3) point higher, as is frequently possible.

If you are not already on a plane but the gust is sufficient to get you on one, the above sequence still applies but with the difference that in step (2) you must bear away quite a bit and give the sail a pump or two so to break onto the plane quickly.

Lulls

It is perhaps most difficult to know what to do in a lull. The correct advice for some situations is point fairly high through a lull so that you'll arrive at the next gust sooner than if you had borne away for speed. This is good advice if you can maintain a plane while still pointing fairly high, or if you can't maintain a plane even if you bear away several degrees. In the first case, pointing high and remaining on the plane will indeed get you to the mark and the next puff of wind

quickest. In the second case, when the lull is so severe that you can't maintain the plane by bearing away a few degrees it's best to forget about planing for the moment and point up toward the next puff of wind. There's a third case, however. If you can maintain the plane by bearing away a bit, do so: the extra speed is worth a slightly lower pointing angle.

Chop

The short, steep, small waves set up by the local wind in semi-sheltered waters, e.g. many reservoirs or lakes, are called 'chop'. As you sail along you'll notice unusually rough and smooth patches. When you encounter a smooth you should head up: the better water will allow you the same speed with a higher pointing angle. When you start pounding into a rough spot you should bear away some in order to maintain speed. Look at the water ahead so that you can anticipate the changes in roughness.

As you sail along, the bow of your board will hit waves of varying size and steepness. Whenever you encounter one especially large and steep which could check your speed inordinately, give a quick, powerful pump with your sail and thrust against the board with your back leg. This must be timed to coincide with the impact of the wave against the bow. If properly done, the pump will drive the board past the wave with minimum loss of speed.

Seas

The large (over 2 m) waves generated by the local wind in open water, such as the ocean, a bay or a very large lake, are called 'seas' and present special difficulties to the racing sailor. As you sail up the face and over the top of each wave, the

rush of water resulting from its passage will tend to make you head off and push the board sideways downwind. The way to minimize these effects is to head up and point higher as you climb and crest the wave. Then, as you start down the back of the wave bear away to regain speed. The cycle should continue in a fairly regular rhythm.

For the most part steering through the waves should be kept subtle; the changes in heading should not be large. However, when you meet a breaking wave you must head up more strongly than usual to avoid being swept downwind with the white water. Lift the weather rail a little more so that it rides up over the broken water. After the crest passes, bear away for speed. Very similar technique is required for going out through surf. In very large seas (over 4 m) the waves may be cresting and breaking with so much force that you can't drive through the white water. Look constantly ahead and to windward to spot exceptionally large or steep waves. When you do spot a wave that is likely to break on you, you must avoid it; go around, not through the place where it will break. Tacking is an option but probably not the safest one. Either head up and let the wave break in front you, or bear away, reach past the danger zone and let it break behind you. Only experience in rough conditions will teach you to predict if, when and where a wave will peak or break.

Putting it together

When you practice sailing upwind you should first concentrate on handling the gusts properly. Experience on flat water and in gusty offshore winds will speed your learning. Second, concentrate solely on weaving through choppy or rough seas and ignore wind variations. Sailing in a place with steady wind and rough water will facilitate this lesson. Finally, try to synthesize your new skills so that they compliment each other. This last step is, of course, the most complex. There will be times when a gust hits just as you encounter an especially rough patch of water; you have to decide just how much you can point up and just how much you have to drive through the chop. There will be times when the wind and seas are from different directions so that you may have to respond more to the wind on one tack, to the seas on the other. Many hours on the water will teach you how to handle all the conditions you may encounter.

Railing
The tendency of the board to rise up uncontrollably on its leeward rail is called 'railing'. Too big a sail or centreboard is frequently the cause, but poor technique can contribute. With the rig tilted strongly to windward, the downward thrust of the mast tends to turn the board over. Also, much of your weight is hanging on the boom rather than being on the windward rail of the board so with little weight on it the edge tends to rise. The way to correct this problem is to hold the rig as vertical as possible.

If you are railing because your centreboard is too big, either sweep it back a few degrees or pull it up vertically in the well 8–10 cm. Either will help control railing, but the second way is better.

Mark rounding
I've already mentioned that the mast should be forward and the centreboard down for sailing upwind. On the last reach before a windward leg,

remain in full-speed reaching trim until within a board length of the mark, then bank the board with your back leg into a smooth carving turn upwind. As you pass the mark release the mast track with your front foot and allow the mast foot to shoot forward. Next, swing the centreboard down and trim out for sailing upwind. It's very important to move the mast foot first and the centreboard only after you've headed up and slowed down a lot.

Close-reaching
Close-reaching, with the centreboard partially down and the mast foot halfway forward, is probably the dullest of all points of sailing: it isn't tactically interesting the way beating and running are, and it isn't especially fast and exciting like beam and broad reaching. Nevertheless it's an important part of the Euro-Funboard Course and should be mastered.

Stance
For close-reaching your stance should be much as for beating,

though you should be farther back. Your front arm should be straight and the back one somewhat bent. In fact, the same is true for all courses except running. Your back leg should be just about straight, the front one slightly bent.

Trim
The board should be bow-down for maximum planing surface and so the stern doesn't sink and create excess drag. Moving the mast forward accomplishes this. Narrow-tail boards will require the mast farther forward than wide-tail boards, and closer reaches will need it farther forward than broader ones.

The board will plane most efficiently when it is heeled neither to windward nor to leeward. However, to smoothly negotiate the seas slapping at the windward bow that rail should be lifted slightly, especially when plowing into cresting waves. Varying the amount the centreboard is down can help control heeling. If the board feels sluggish, dead in the water, and you can't fetch

the next mark without digging the windward rail in, swing a little more blade down: you'll plane more efficiently and point higher.

If, on the other hand, you're having no problem pointing toward the next mark but you are having a problem with the board wanting to railride, simply swing the blade back a little until you can easily sail on an even keel. In general, use as little centreboard as possible because it creates drag, but as much as you need to point to the next mark.

You'll want to have at least your back foot in a strap and if possible your front foot also. Quite often my back foot will go into one of the forward reaching straps, while my front foot uses the upwind one.

Gusts and lulls
The traditional advice for handling variations in wind strength while reaching is: head up in the lulls, bear away in the gusts. That advice doesn't apply to a sailboard on a close reach. In the lulls you'll want to maintain a fast plane and bearing away slightly usually achieves that. In the gusts you can maintain good speed while pointing a bit higher. The gust allows you to point higher because initially it frees your apparent wind, and this makes you go faster which in turn causes your centreboard and skeg to generate more lift. Also, since there will be a slight tendency to railride in the gusts, heading up will control that.

Aim to trim so that you head a little above the mark in the gusts and a little below it in the lulls, with your net direction of travel towards the mark. If you're heading directly at the mark in the gusts and a little below it in the lulls, you should probably swing your centreboard down just a little bit more.

Waves
You should handle waves much the same way as when closehauled. Bear away and drive through the rough spots so that they don't slow you down; take a bite to windward in the smooth spots. Look out for cresting or breaking waves and don't let them push you downwind.

Beam-reaching
Reaching on a course below that which requires the centreboard to be down, but is at more than 100° to the true wind, is a faster point of sailing than close-reaching and less stiffling tactically.

Stance
Your arms will be the same as for other points of sailing but your legs will be different. The farther off the wind, the more your back leg is likely to be bent and your front leg straight.

Both feet should be in straps unless the wind is fairly light. In that case, when getting your weight forward and trying to maintain a plane is the prime consideration, ignore the straps or just slide a foot loosely into one so that you're anchored to the board. Normally you'll be moving fast enough that you'll want to be in the straps. You'll probably use the more forward of your reaching straps. In mild conditions your feet can be fairly close together so that your weight is divided fairly evenly between them. It's not an especially fast way to sail, but it prevents early fatigue of one leg.

To get maximum speed in rough conditions your feet should be spread wide. Your back leg may tire quickly, but you'll be better able to control the pitching of the board as well as its tendency to fly up into the air.

Trim
The board should be flat, heeled neither to windward nor to leeward. Fore-and-aft trim should take care of itself; if you're heading fairly high your weight should be more forward and the bow not too high in the air; if you're more off the wind your weight should be back more and the bow higher.

One situation that affects hull trim, not only on a beam reach but on all points of sailing, is very strong wind. Over Force 6 or 7 it can catch under the windward rail, lift a board off the water and blow it downwind. To keep on the water and in control you must tilt the windward rail down; the wind will not be able to get under the rail and lift, but will instead push the board down.

Gusts and lulls
It's best to follow the traditional advice of heading up in the lulls and off in the gusts if you're having no trouble pointing high enough to fetch the next mark. If the reach is so tight that you might not quite fetch the mark, handle the gusts the same way you would if your blade were partially down: head up and take a bite to windward during the gusts and bear away slightly to maintain speed through the lulls.

Waves
Frequently your course will be angled into the waves, causing a tendency to leave the water. Getting air may be fun but it's not fast. Avoid jumps in the following ways.

Try to steer so that you don't hit the steepest waves, or at least not the steepest part of each wave. You have to look well ahead and recognize in advance waves that may cause trouble when you get to them. A slight change of course up or down

wind will usually steer around the worst spots.

Bend and straighten your legs so they act like shock absorbers. As the board lifts over a wave bend your knees, then as the wave passes straighten them. Energy that is not expended in raising your body an extra few inches is available to make the board go faster. If you get partially airborne pull the tail sharply up and to windward with your legs. Doing so will get it back on the water quickly and reduce the tendency to head up. Heading up even slightly while partially or entirely in the air is very damaging to speed. Beside the risk of spinning out, you are sure to land slightly sideways and out of trim.

Bearing away slightly as you approach and traverse a crest will reduce the steepness of the ramp and greatly diminish your changes of getting air. If you miscalculate badly or for some other reason find yourself about to get a good (bad) jump, luff the sail. Unless you're very good, luffing for a moment will be faster more often than jumping.

It's possible to get air and go fast also, but it's difficult and risky. If you get a small jump and don't want to luff, 'lock' your body into the position it was in when you took off, bear away very slightly and keep the board parallel with the water. The object is to go through the air as if you are still on the water, so that when you do hit the water again you're in perfect trim. Your landing should be basically flat with the bow touching just an instant before the stern. This will cushion the landing adequately without hurting your speed. A tail-first landing will slow you down.

Pumping in choppy waves, Ken pulls in the sail several times to get onto a small wave.

Pounding

Sometimes on both beam and broad reaches the board will tend to pitch up and down and pound the bow into the water. Pounding causes the angle to the water to change drastically, makes the stern dig in when the bow is up and generally causes excess drag. Flat boards pound more than ones with a moderate Vee, and on both types it's very difficult to control. Sailing with your feet widely spread out fore-and-aft helps.

Broad-reaching

The one thing that most characterizes broad-reaching is *speed*. Pure speed over the water is the objective and the reward of this point of sailing.

Stance

Your back leg should be bent and your back foot in the aft strap. If winds are light or the reach especially broad you'll have to stand forward more, and may not even need the straps. But on a high-speed broad-reach you need to be back on the board and have both feet firmly in the straps. You'll also be rather bent at the waist.

Gusts and lulls

'Down in the gusts, up in the lulls' definitely applies on this point of sailing. When a gust hits you can stay in it longer if you bear away, and you can go even faster when more off the wind. When the gust eases it's best to head up to maintain speed (too broad a reach, just like too close a reach, is slow) and to reduce the time it takes for the next gust to reach you. In flat water this rule should be followed religiously. In rough water your position with respect to the waves will contribute to deciding whether to head up or bear away.

Waves

Surfing the swell is what makes broad-reaching most interesting. Working the waves perfectly is very difficult, but the payoff is dramatically better speed. The trick is to bear away in front of a swell so that you're sailing downhill for as long as possible. Then, as it passes under you head up to maintain speed and watch for a chance to bear away in front of another swell.

To pick the best waves don't look back at what's coming but ahead at what has just gone past. If the wave which has just passed you is steep on the back side and has a deep trough behind it, bear away and point your bow into that trough. Continue to steer into the deepest part of the trough and you can't go wrong.

When you sense that you can no longer keep up with the trough in front of you, don't wait to slow down too much and definitely don't drop off the plane. Instead head up to a higher, faster sailing angle and look for another trough to chase.

There are frequently two or more wave trains coming at one time, a large swell and smaller chop driven by the local wind, possibly in another direction. You should be aware of both wave patterns and concentrate on surfing one or the other whenever your course is appropriate. You can bear away in a gust and surf the locally generated waves, then as the gust eases or the wave passes head up and work the larger swell.

Where two waves intersect there will be an extra large and steep peak which moves in the direction of neither system but somewhere between. These peaks are not usually long-lived but they can still be useful in propelling you in the desired direction; they can also be exceptionally powerful.

Pumping

The International Sailboarders Association rules agree that pumping is legal in World Cup racing. In fact, most pros would say that pumping is a vital and integral part of windsurfing, and there are times when it is useful even though one isn't racing. So it is necessary to learn how to pump effectively.

There are two types of pump, *arm pump* and *body pump*. The arm pump consists of a small, quick back-and-forth motion of the sail, frequently followed immediately by more of the same. It is useful in several situations: when pounding into chop while sailing upwind (as mentioned before); to provide a little extra push to stay on a wave that you're surfing; and to help 'feel' the sail when you're in a lull or not sheeted in correctly.

Since windsurfers don't look at telltales on the sail to see if they are trimmed correctly, they must instead feel the sail. High aspect ratio sails are especially difficult to trim correctly, so one often doesn't know whether he's in a lull or if the sail is just stalled. A quick arm pump or two will provide the needed information and, if the sail is stalled, will help to accelerate the stagnant air flow.

Body pumps are used when you need a big boost of acceleration. They involve a large, relatively slow, movement of the sail and a large expenditure of energy: I have finished the end of broad reach quite exhausted from pumping. As the photos show, you use the entire body – bending at the waist and straightening – to give the pump maximum range of motion and force.

Don't pump indiscriminately. Pumping at the wrong time or in the wrong way will do as much harm as good, so try to use it as precisely as a good jockey uses his whip. Only through experience and practice, however, can you learn to pump well.

Plunging

One great danger on a broad reach is what I call 'plunging' – allowing the bow to plunge or drive into the back of a slow-moving wave. A slight plunge can slow you down, while a bad one can cause you to fall. Take care against this error by looking ahead at the water and steering around the steepest wave backs. If you can't avoid a plunge by steering, push down sharply with your back leg and pull up on the boom: you should thereby be able to mitigate the plunge or avoid it entirely.

If you're sailing well you'll be using both techniques all the time in order to keep the forward half of your board from striking the water with more force and frequency than necessary.

Mark rounding

At the start of the reach you must round the weather mark and adjust your mast track and centreboard. It's best to luff the sail momentarily while you swing the centreboard up, then sheet in and bear away several degrees before pulling the mast back. You must luff the sail in order to swing the centreboard back because of the side force that locks the blade in place whenever the sail is full. The broader the reach you're sailing on the easier it is to pull the mast back.

Tacking

Tacking a World Cup type of racing board is more difficult than on any other big board; it is slow to turn into the wind because of the large skeg, and one has to cover a lot of distance to go all the way around the mast in its forward position. The photos show a tacking technique which emphasizes speed and safety.

Gybing

There are two main techniques which you should know, the carved type and the pivot type of gybe.

The Carved Gybe You can go into a mark rounding at full speed, hold good speed through the turn and fill away on the other gybe without having dropped off the plane. This is the gybe to use whenever possible.

The Pivot Gybe should be used in very rough conditions when you're not confident of being able to execute a good carving gybe, or in light conditions when there isn't enough wind to power you completely through a carving gybe. The pivot is also useful in some tactical situations, e.g. capsized boards could leave you room for a tight sharp turn but not enough for a wide sweeping one. The pivot gybe is the obvious choice.

STRATEGY AND TACTICS

The art of developing a master plan for a race is strategy. It includes deciding whether to cover a particular opponent, judging whether there is likely to be a favored side to the beat and how to play it, whether to go high or low on a reach, whether the current is of significant strength and if so how to use it.

Whether strategy is of great or little importance in a race depends much on the course sailed. Euro-Funboard courses, for example, have such a short windward leg and such short close reaches that there are few strategic options during a race. Hence strategy is of little importance. On the World Cup course, however, since there is more windward work and the reaches are longer and broader, the sailor has ample opportunity to gain advantage through superior strategy.

Racing strategies common to other sailing craft are also applicable to windsurfers. Since the topic is well covered in dinghy racing books I'll discuss here only those strategic situations unique to World Cup type racing.

Rule Number One

Your highest priority is to stay on your feet, so your main strategy through every part of every race is to avoid situations and actions that could put you in the water. Prior to the race check the wind and be sure you have a sail that isn't too big. At the start, if your board handling is poor or the fleet especially aggressive, or the conditions are particularly rough, keep away from the crowded parts of the line and concentrate on getting off without a crash. On the weather leg look well ahead and anticipate tactical situations, such as crossing behind a starboard tacker, to avoid collisions or hurried manoeuvres which might make you fall. Be careful and deliberate in adjusting your centreboard and mast, and avoid sailing into crowds or rafts of capsized boards. Following this advice will help you achieve your first strategic objective – not falling in.

Starting

Your highest priority here (beside not falling) is to start in such a way that you will be able to head for the favored side of the beat immediately. Since windsurfers are so fast, and point relatively low, it's a disaster to be heading in the wrong direction: small wind shifts can mean large gains for those who play them correctly.

Beating

World Cup boards are fast through the water but relatively slow to come about, so tacking should be done as seldom as possible. On Euro-Funboard courses, which frequently have a very short weather leg, it is sometimes possible and wise to tack only once on the beat. So consideration of the amount of speed lost through tacking is a major factor in deciding on the favored side of the beat. If the wind and current don't favour one side, then the favoured side is that which requires fewest tacks.

Reaching

Beam and broad reaches, especially long ones, require one to decide whether to sail high, low or to stay on the direct line. Aside from tactical considerations, wind and current variations along the reach determine the fastest course to take. If the wind is stronger near the end of the reach it's usually best to sail above the rhumb line so that you can bear away for more speed in the stronger wind. This advice is standard for most types of boat. However, if the course is a beam reach or higher, and the wind is light but stronger at the end of the reach, it may pay to sail below the rhumb line. By bearing away to a course slightly below the rhumb line initially, you can maintain a faster plane in the lighter wind than you could if you pointed directly for the mark. Then, as the wind increases down the reach you can head up toward the mark without loosing speed.

Tactics

The art of manoeuvring to gain positional advantage over opponents, in order to secure those objectives designated by strategy, is tactics. If at the start you make the strategic decision that the right side of the beat is favored, you will have to tack onto port to get there. Suppose you're sailing away from the starting line on starboard and there's a board just behind and a little to windward of you preventing you from tacking onto port. You now have to make the tactical decision of how to get onto port without fouling the guy behind you, and you have to make it quickly: every second spent on starboard puts you farther behind the boards already on port tack. Your options, in order of preference, are:

(1) Sail faster and point higher so that the other guy falls directly behind you or tacks to clear his air. You can then tack.

(2) Hail him: tell him the right side is favored and that you should both tack. If he's smart, or if he thinks you're smart, he'll take your suggestion.

(3) Luff and let him pass.

In any case, if you know that the right side is favored make whatever tactical manoeuvres are necessary to get over there.

Beating

In a close crossing situation port tackers should never consider tacking into a safe leeward position on a starboard tack board. Since World Cup boards are so slow to tack it's very difficult to time the turn so that it is effective: (1) the starboard tacker usually sails past the tacking board before the tack is finished, and (2) the starboard tacker has enough warning of the tacking board's intentions (by the slowness of the tack) that he can take evasive action. In order for this manoeuvre to work the tacking board must be two or three, perhaps more, board lengths ahead of the starboard tack board, in which case the crossing would not be close.

Port tackers should look ahead, identify close crossing situations early and take early steps, either pinching, footing or pumping, to avoid a foul. Bearing away early and smoothly to pass astern of a starboard tack board is the safest thing to do.

Reaching

On a reach, if someone else is faster don't try to luff him but instead bear away and let him pass with least disturbance to your wind. An attempt to luff him could only be successful if he came so close that you were able to head up quickly and make contact. That could damage your back, but could also put him in the water.

Exactly such a situation occured during the 1983 San Francisco World Cup. G6 was overtaking me on a broad reach while I was trying to decide whether to pass another board to windward or to leeward. I had looked very briefly over my shoulder to ascertain the threat from that quarter and decided to head up and protect my inside position at the next mark. The thought was followed immediately by the action. This, however, caught G6, who was to windward and overtaking, by surprise. As I headed up at 20 knots the bow of his board glanced across my back. The contact caused G6 to explode into a ball of spray and ripped Mylar. It's against the racing rules to do something like that intentionally, but it is the responsibility of the overtaking and windward yacht to keep clear in such a situation.

On a close reach, if someone faster is trying to pass you can hold him off by pointing high and giving him your dirty air. If he breaks to windward and ahead of your dirty air, bear away some for speed until he starts to take your wind, then head up as you fall behind so as to clear your wind. On the other hand, if he tries to pass to leeward bear away and give him dirty air for as long as possible, then if he gets by anyway head up again to keep out of his bad air.

If you're fast and know it, and have a lot of boards to pass, it's usually best to head high at the start of the reach so that you can blast by the herd with little opposition. If, on the other hand, you're slow on a reach there's little you can do tactically; just concentrate on keeping your air clear and sailing as fast as you can.

Mark rounding

Your best approach to a gybe mark whether you're ahead or behind is to start your turn downwind from well to weather of the mark, and to finish the gybe close to leeward of the mark. Thus, if ahead, you lessen the chance of the board behind cutting inside and stealing your wind as you try to accelerate on the next reach. If behind, you position yourself so that if your gybe is cleaner, smoother and quicker you'll be in a position to accelerate past the board ahead as you start the next leg. In either case a smooth carving gybe is best. However, if you're ahead and forced to start your gybe close to windward of the mark, a tight, quick pivot gybe is best. The board behind will still gain, but won't be able to pass.

How could you be forced to start your turn from close to windward of the mark, you might wonder? The board astern might try to gain an inside overlap as you approach the mark, thus forcing you to bear away defensively for more speed. Once he has forced you to bear away, he can head up and prepare for a perfect gybe while your approach is marred by his feint. Your defence is to be aware that his move to the inside may be only a feint, and to head up quickly as soon as the threat of his gaining an inside overlap is gone.

Should the board behind gain the right to buoy room, you must head up sharply just before rounding and prepare to make a carving gybe, while your opponent is forced by his inside position to make a pivot gybe. If your execution is better and you are able to cut inside and steal his wind, you can regain the lead.

There are innumerable tactical and strategic situations, and if you're an active racer you'll probably find yourself in most of them at some time. Your best source of information on tactics and strategy remains the books about traditional yacht and dinghy racing.*

*See pages 118–19, listing windsurfing books including *Windsurfing Race Tactics* by Noel Swanson.

WINDSURFING RACING TECHNIQUE
Philip Pudenz and Karl Messmer

Two of the world's top sailors analyse, explain and demonstrate the techniques needed for race winning – fast tacking and gybing, speed, mark rounding, 720° turns, trapezing, sail/board trim,

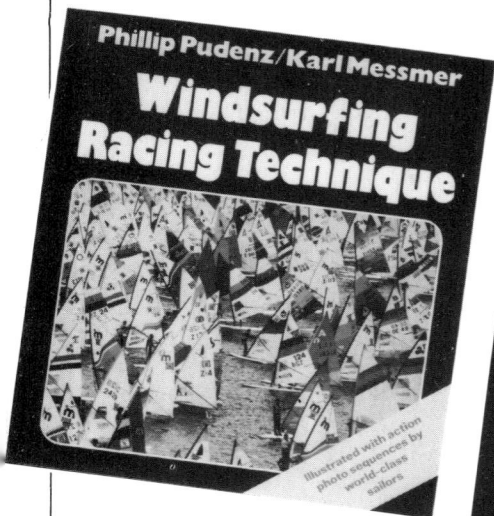

starts, tactics and picking the best courses.

Racing courses, signals, scoring, protests and the racing rules particular to windsurfing are all covered, so getting started in racing, or improving your results, are made easier.

Dozens of colour and black/white photos and sequences by Michael Garff make this a unique book.

Hardback, 180 pages

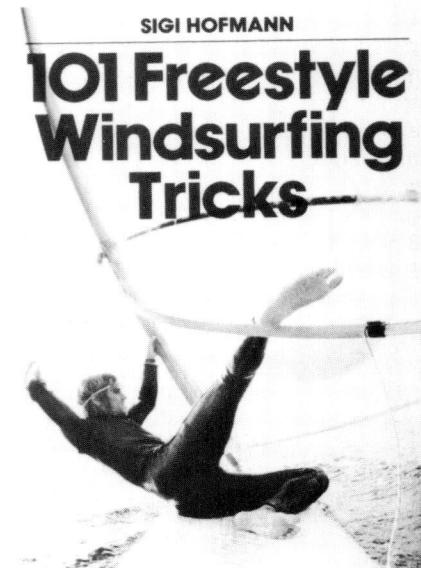

WINDSURFING TECHNIQUE
Niko Stickl and Michael Garff

A unique approach, using photomontage and sequence pictures, with plenty of spectacular colour shots of world-class sailors in action. Starting from the basic stance and manoeuvres, and with detailed analysis and instruction taking you up to advanced sailing techniques, this is the book for improving your performance.

Hardback, 180 pages

101 FREESTYLE WINDSURFING TRICKS
Sigi Hofmann

Starting with preparatory exercises, and using series photography and a breakdown of each trick into its component moves, this book makes it possible to begin with the easier ones and work up to the most daring and spectacular. The stunts here are graded according to difficulty and wind strength, and arranged in a logical sequence so that you build on the techniques already learned.

With many good tips on competition and building a freestyle programme, by one of the top international sailors.

Paperback, 120 pages

SAILBOARDS CUSTOM-MADE
Hans Fichtner and Michael Garff

Do-it-yourself sailboard building is a practical, economical way of having a 'fun board' for the kids to learn on, or to try out your own ideas. Hans Fichtner is a shaper for Mistral and here describes the methods and tools that are most suitable for amateur builders and will give a satisfying, quality result. 8 pages of colour board graphics.
Paperback, 120 pages

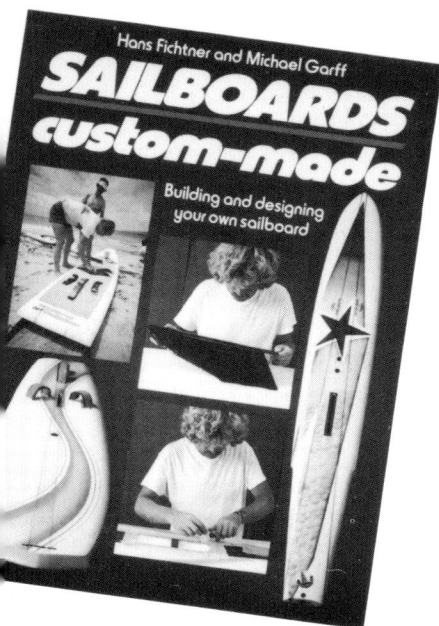

WINDSURFING RACE TACTICS
Noel Swanson

A forthcoming title in the Stanford Maritime windsurfing list.

A very comprehensive, fully illustrated analysis of all the various board-against board situations that occur in racing. The tactical problems of starts, upwind legs, mark rounding, reaching and downwind legs, and finishing are all analysed, along with the relevant Racing Rules, and the best possible courses and manoeuvres that are allowed. There is also advice on broader strategy for pre-start manoeuvres, the different legs of a course, changes in wind and tide, and on the physical and mental preparation for racing.

FASTER BETTER WINDSURFING
Uwe Preuss, Jochen Taaks and Sepp Winbeck

The latest methods for faster learning, using correct sailing techniques from the very start so that you improve faster and get a sound basis for funboard and advanced sailing. Based on the highly successful teaching system of the German Association of Windsurfing Schools (VDWS).
Photo sequences help explain basic and advanced tacking and gybing, trapeze techniques, carved turns, beach and water starts. The text also covers essential background on equipment, racing, collision avoidance and rights-of-way, tides and currents, rescue and emergency repairs.
Paperback, 122 pages

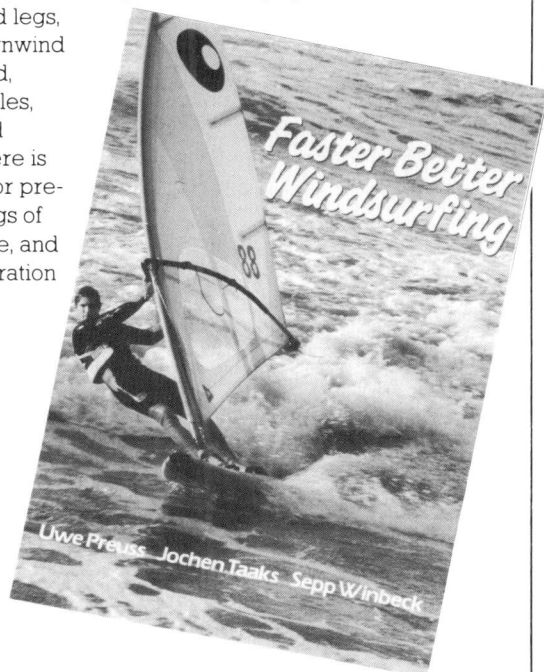

STANFORD MARITIME
Member Company of the George Philip Group
12 Long Acre, London WC2E 9LP, U.K.